Emotional Intelligence & Inner Child Healing: The Complete Collection for Deeper Self-Awareness and Emotional Freedom

Grace Hartwell

Table of contents

Introduction: Begin the Healing

There are moments in life when something feels off, even if nothing on the surface appears wrong. A relationship ends in the same painful way it always has. A moment of criticism at work lingers for days longer than it should. A small conflict triggers a reaction that seems far larger than the situation itself. Many people respond to these moments by trying to think their way through them. They analyze what happened, replay conversations, or promise themselves they will behave differently next time. Sometimes this helps for a while, but often the same patterns return. The reaction comes back, the fear resurfaces, and the familiar emotional cycle repeats.

What remains hidden for many people is that these reactions are rarely created in the moment. They are echoes of something older.

Human beings learn emotional patterns long before they understand what emotions are. Childhood is the first training ground for how we experience safety, connection, worth, and belonging. During those early years, the nervous system absorbs information constantly. A child learns what love feels like, how conflict is handled, whether mistakes are safe or dangerous, and whether emotions are welcomed or ignored. These lessons are rarely taught through words. They are transmitted through tone of voice, facial expressions, consistency, absence, and countless everyday interactions.

Over time, these experiences shape emotional expectations about the world.

A child who receives warmth and reassurance during difficult moments begins to associate vulnerability with safety. A child whose emotions are dismissed or punished may learn that feelings must be hidden. A child who grows up around unpredictability may develop constant alertness, scanning the environment for signs of danger. None of these patterns form because a child consciously chooses them. They develop because the developing mind is trying to survive, adapt, and make sense of its surroundings.

The remarkable strength of the human mind is its ability to adapt. The hidden cost of that strength is that adaptations formed in childhood often remain active long after the original environment has disappeared.

By adulthood, these patterns can shape nearly every important area of life. They influence the partners people choose, the way they respond to criticism, how comfortable they feel expressing needs, and how they react to emotional closeness. They can affect career decisions, risk tolerance, boundaries, and self-confidence. In many cases, the individual does not recognize the pattern itself. They only experience the consequences: repeated relationship conflicts, difficulty trusting others, an internal voice that constantly questions their worth, or a persistent feeling of emotional distance from themselves.

This is where emotional blind spots begin.

An emotional blind spot is not simply a lack of knowledge. It is a pattern that operates automatically, often outside conscious awareness. People may recognize the outcome of the pattern but not the underlying emotional logic that drives it. Someone might say, "I don't know why I always shut down when conversations get serious," or "I don't understand why I push people away when they get too close." These questions are not signs of weakness. They are signals pointing toward unfinished emotional learning.

Behind many of these blind spots lives something psychologists often refer to as the inner child.

The inner child is not a metaphor for immaturity. It represents the emotional experiences, needs, and memories that formed during the earliest stages of development. Even when people grow into capable adults, parts of their emotional world can remain tied to those early moments of vulnerability. A rejection in adulthood may unconsciously activate the same feelings a child experienced when they felt ignored or misunderstood. A conflict may awaken the same fear that once accompanied raised voices in the household.

When this happens, the adult mind may know that the present situation is manageable, but the emotional system reacts as if the past has returned.

This is why emotional intelligence and inner child healing cannot be separated. Emotional intelligence provides the skills to recognize, regulate, and communicate feelings. Inner child work helps identify where those feelings originally formed and why they still carry such intensity. Without emotional awareness, childhood wounds remain hidden and continue to influence behavior. Without compassion for those wounds, emotional insight can become harsh self-criticism rather than healing.

Many people attempt one side of this process without the other.

Some pursue awareness through books, reflection, or therapy. They begin to recognize patterns and can even explain their emotional triggers in detail. Yet awareness alone does not always lead to change. A person might know that their fear of abandonment comes from early experiences, but still feel overwhelmed when closeness appears in the present.

Others focus primarily on healing techniques such as affirmations, visualization, or self-care rituals. These practices can offer temporary comfort, but without emotional skill the underlying patterns remain fragile. When life becomes stressful again, the old reactions quickly return.

The core thesis of this book is simple but powerful: awareness without compassion is incomplete, and healing without emotional skill is unstable.

Real transformation requires both.

Understanding the origins of emotional patterns provides clarity. Compassion allows those patterns to soften rather than tighten under judgment. Emotional intelligence supplies the tools to navigate feelings in real time. When these elements work together, something remarkable begins to happen. The past loses some of its power over the present. Reactions become choices. Relationships begin to feel safer and more authentic. Self-worth stops depending entirely on external validation.

Healing, in this sense, is not about erasing the past. It is about integrating it.

Integration means acknowledging that the younger versions of ourselves were responding to circumstances with the tools they had available. It means recognizing that many behaviors that once served a protective function may no longer be necessary. It also means learning new emotional responses that support connection, resilience, and self-respect.

This process does not happen overnight, and it does not require perfection.

The purpose of this book is not to offer a quick fix or a single insight that changes everything instantly. Instead, it offers a path—a structured journey that combines understanding with practice. Each stage of the journey builds on the previous one, allowing change to unfold gradually and sustainably.

The first part of the book focuses on emotional foundations. Before deep healing can occur, it is essential to understand how emotions function and why they exist. Many people grow up receiving confusing messages about feelings. Some are told to suppress them, others are overwhelmed by them, and many simply never learn how to interpret them. This section clarifies what emotions actually do and how emotional intelligence transforms them from sources of chaos into valuable sources of information.

Once this foundation is established, the book turns toward childhood experiences and the emotional imprints they leave behind. This stage does not aim to assign blame or dwell endlessly on the past. Instead, it encourages careful observation. Readers learn how to identify recurring emotional patterns and trace them back to the environments where they first developed. By recognizing these connections, previously confusing reactions begin to make sense.

Understanding opens the door, but it is only the beginning.

The next stage introduces practical healing tools. These exercises are designed to strengthen emotional regulation, self-compassion, and inner safety. They help readers reconnect with parts of themselves that may have been ignored, criticized, or silenced for years. Through repeated practice, these tools gradually transform emotional reactions that once felt automatic.

As healing deepens, relationships naturally come into focus. Much of human pain occurs in connection with others, and much of healing also happens there. This section explores how childhood patterns influence adult relationships, including communication styles, boundaries, attachment dynamics, and conflict responses. Readers learn how to shift these patterns so that relationships become spaces of growth rather than repetition.

Finally, the book addresses long-term integration. Emotional growth is not a single breakthrough moment but an ongoing process of awareness, reflection, and practice. The final chapters help readers develop habits that maintain emotional resilience over time. Instead of returning to old cycles, they build a framework for continued development and self-understanding.

By the time readers reach the first chapter, they will not be asked to change everything at once. They will simply be invited to begin paying attention.

Attention is where healing starts.

When people begin to observe their emotional world with curiosity instead of judgment, patterns that once seemed permanent start to shift. Small moments of awareness accumulate. Reactions slow down. New choices become possible. The inner child that once operated from fear begins to experience something different: recognition, patience, and care.

This is the beginning of healing.

Not a dramatic transformation that happens overnight, but a quiet and steady movement toward wholeness. Each insight builds understanding. Each practice strengthens emotional skill. Each moment of compassion repairs something that may have been neglected for years.

The journey ahead is both personal and practical. It asks readers to reflect, experiment, and remain open to new perspectives about themselves. At times the process may feel uncomfortable, because growth often involves meeting parts of ourselves we once avoided. Yet it is precisely in those moments that the greatest breakthroughs occur.

You do not need to arrive at this journey with perfect self-knowledge or emotional control. You only need a willingness to explore.

The work begins with a simple question: what patterns have shaped your emotional life, and what might become possible if you understood them differently?

The chapters that follow will help you answer that question step by step.

Chapter 1 — See Your Patterns

1.1 The Invisible Loops That Shape Your Life

Most people believe their reactions come from the present moment. A harsh comment hurts because it was unfair. A conflict becomes overwhelming because the situation escalated. A sudden wave of anxiety appears because something stressful happened that day. On the surface, this explanation feels logical. Life happens, and emotions respond.

Yet if you pause and look closely at your experiences across months or years, something interesting begins to appear. Certain situations trigger almost identical reactions every time. The names of the people may change. The circumstances may look different. But the emotional response feels strangely familiar.

You might notice that criticism affects you far more deeply than it seems to affect others. Perhaps you withdraw from conversations when they become emotionally intense. Maybe you feel a strong need to prove your value whenever your work is evaluated. Or you might find yourself repeatedly choosing partners who are distant, unavailable, or unpredictable.

At first these experiences seem like separate events. But when viewed together, they begin to form a pattern.

A pattern is not just a repeated behavior. It is a learned emotional pathway that has become so familiar that it runs almost automatically. It shapes how you interpret events, how you respond to people, and how you protect yourself from perceived threats.

Patterns rarely feel like patterns from the inside. They simply feel like "the way things happen."

Imagine someone who feels intense anxiety when receiving feedback at work. They may tell themselves that the anxiety exists because the workplace is demanding. That explanation may contain some truth. But if the same anxiety appears with every supervisor, in every organization, and in every type of evaluation, something deeper may be happening.

The mind is not responding only to the current situation. It is responding to a long-standing emotional script.

These scripts often develop early in life. Childhood is the period when the brain learns how to interpret safety, belonging, approval, and rejection. During those years, the emotional system is constantly scanning the environment and drawing conclusions about what actions lead to connection and what actions lead to pain.

If expressing feelings was ignored or discouraged, a child might learn that emotional openness is unsafe. If mistakes were met with criticism or disappointment, the child may begin to associate errors with shame rather than learning. If attention and affection appeared unpredictably, the child might grow highly sensitive to signs of rejection.

None of these conclusions are made consciously. They are built gradually through repeated experiences. The brain is simply trying to predict what will happen next so it can protect itself.

Over time, these predictions turn into habits.

A child who learns that vulnerability leads to embarrassment may become an adult who avoids difficult conversations. Someone who felt responsible for keeping peace in a chaotic household might grow into an adult who struggles to set boundaries. Another person may have learned that achievement was the primary path to recognition and therefore feels constant pressure to perform.

These behaviors once had a purpose. They helped the younger version of you navigate the emotional environment you lived in.

The challenge appears when those same strategies continue operating long after the original circumstances have changed.

Consider how quickly emotional reactions can occur. A comment from a partner might trigger defensiveness before you even have time to think. A slight delay in a message might lead to a surge of insecurity. A disagreement might cause your mind to jump immediately to worst-case scenarios.

These reactions can feel sudden and uncontrollable. But in most cases they are not random. They are learned responses traveling along well-established neural pathways.

Think of these pathways as emotional shortcuts. When the brain recognizes a familiar situation, it immediately activates the response that has been practiced the most. The process happens so quickly that conscious reasoning often arrives after the reaction has already begun.

This is why patterns feel automatic.

The goal of this chapter is not to eliminate those reactions instantly. That would be unrealistic and unnecessarily harsh. Instead, the goal is to develop the first and most important skill in emotional growth: honest observation.

Observation means learning to notice your reactions without immediately judging them or trying to suppress them. It means becoming curious about the patterns that repeat in your life rather than assuming they are permanent parts of your personality.

Many people struggle with this step because they confuse observation with criticism.

When someone begins noticing their patterns, they may quickly move into self-judgment. They might say, "Why am I always like this?" or "I should be stronger than this." But harsh judgment rarely leads to meaningful change. It usually reinforces the very patterns that caused the reaction in the first place.

Real observation looks different. It sounds more like quiet curiosity.

You might start asking questions such as: What situations tend to trigger my strongest emotional reactions? When I feel hurt, do I tend to withdraw, attack, or seek reassurance? Are there conversations I consistently avoid? What fears appear repeatedly in my relationships or work?

These questions do not require immediate answers. Their purpose is simply to open awareness.

Awareness gradually reveals the loops that operate beneath daily behavior.

One common loop involves avoidance. A person may feel uncomfortable expressing disagreement, so they stay silent. Because they stay silent, their needs remain unmet. Over time resentment grows, which eventually leads to emotional distance or sudden outbursts. After the conflict occurs, the person may feel regret and promise themselves to avoid similar situations in the future. Ironically, that promise often leads them back to silence, restarting the same cycle.

Another pattern appears in the search for approval. Someone who learned early in life that praise brought safety may become highly sensitive to evaluation. They work harder and harder to prove their value, but the relief that comes from recognition rarely lasts long. The next challenge quickly triggers the same pressure to succeed.

Some patterns revolve around emotional withdrawal. When closeness begins to feel intense, the person distances themselves. This distance may provide temporary relief, but it also prevents deeper connection. As relationships weaken, the individual may feel lonely or misunderstood, which reinforces the belief that intimacy is difficult or unreliable.

None of these loops exist because a person is weak or flawed. They exist because the emotional system is trying to protect itself using strategies that once worked.

The difficulty is that protective strategies can eventually become limiting ones.

When a reaction occurs automatically, it leaves very little room for choice. The brain moves along the familiar path before conscious reflection has time to intervene. This is why people often say things like, "I don't know why I reacted that way," or "I wish I had handled that differently."

Observation slows this process down.

The moment you begin noticing a pattern, you create a small space between the trigger and the reaction. That space may only last a few seconds at first, but it is incredibly powerful. Within that brief pause lies the possibility of responding differently.

Think of it as turning on a light in a room that was previously dark. The furniture was always there, but you could not see it clearly before. Once the light is on, you begin to understand the layout of the space.

Self-observation works the same way.

At first you may only notice patterns after they happen. You might look back at a conversation and realize that you shut down the moment it became emotional. Later you might begin noticing the reaction while it is happening. Eventually you may start recognizing the early signals that appear just before the pattern activates.

These signals often show up in the body before they appear in thoughts. A tightening in the chest, a sudden rush of heat, a sense of pressure in the stomach, or a strong urge to escape the situation can all indicate that an emotional pattern is beginning to activate.

Learning to recognize these signals is one of the most valuable skills in emotional growth. They act as early warning signs that something deeper is being triggered.

When those signals appear, the most helpful response is not immediate action but curiosity. Instead of reacting automatically, you might ask yourself a simple question: what does this feeling remind me of?

Sometimes the answer will be obvious. Other times it may take patience and reflection. But even asking the question begins to loosen the grip of automatic behavior.

Over time, patterns that once felt invisible start to become clear. You may notice that certain fears repeat across different relationships. You may recognize that your reaction to authority figures echoes feelings you experienced long ago. You might discover that the pressure you place on yourself mirrors expectations you internalized years earlier.

This awareness is not meant to create blame or regret about the past. Its purpose is to give you a clearer map of how your emotional system learned to operate.

Once you see the map, new directions become possible.

Before meaningful change can occur, the patterns themselves must become visible. Without awareness, behavior continues on autopilot. With awareness, the same situations become opportunities for learning and adjustment.

This is why the first step in healing is not fixing your emotions but seeing them clearly.

In the chapters that follow, you will explore the deeper origins of these patterns and learn practical tools to reshape them. But none of that work would be effective without the foundation you are beginning to build here.

Honest observation is where transformation starts.

It requires patience, curiosity, and a willingness to look inward without harsh judgment. Yet once this skill develops, it becomes one of the most reliable guides you can have.

Your patterns are not permanent definitions of who you are. They are simply emotional habits that once helped you navigate your world.

And every habit, once seen clearly, can begin to change.

1.2 Understanding the Chain: Triggers, Emotions, Thoughts, and Behaviors

Once you begin observing your patterns, another important layer of understanding becomes possible. Many emotional reactions feel overwhelming not because the situation itself is unbearable, but because several internal processes are happening at the same time. They blend together so quickly that it becomes difficult to distinguish what actually happened from the meaning the mind assigns to it.

To create clarity, it helps to separate four elements that often get tangled together: the trigger, the emotion, the thought, and the behavior.

These elements form a chain that shapes nearly every emotional experience. When the chain is invisible, reactions feel confusing and uncontrollable. When the chain becomes clear, you begin to see where interpretation enters the picture and where new choices become possible.

The first element is the trigger. A trigger is simply the event that activates the reaction. It is what happens externally or internally before the emotional response begins. Sometimes the trigger is obvious, such as a disagreement, a criticism, or an unexpected change in plans. Other times it is subtle, like a tone of voice, a facial expression, or even a memory that appears suddenly in the mind.

Triggers are often neutral events by themselves. Their power comes from the meaning they carry for the person experiencing them.

For example, imagine receiving a short message from a colleague that says, "We need to talk later." For one person, this might simply signal a routine conversation. For another, it may instantly create tension or worry. The message itself has not changed. What changes is the emotional significance attached to it.

After the trigger comes the emotion.

Emotions are immediate responses generated by the nervous system. They arise quickly and often before conscious thinking begins. Feelings such as fear, sadness, anger, disappointment, or shame can appear within seconds of a triggering event. These emotional signals are not problems by themselves. In fact, they serve important functions. Fear alerts us to potential danger. Anger can highlight violated boundaries. Sadness may signal loss or disconnection.

However, emotions rarely remain isolated. Almost immediately, the mind begins constructing explanations about what the emotion means.

This is where thoughts enter the chain.

Thoughts are the interpretations we form about what happened and why it matters. They are the internal narratives that attempt to make sense of our emotional reactions. The mind is constantly searching for patterns and predictions, so it naturally builds stories to explain situations.

For instance, imagine that a friend cancels plans at the last minute. The trigger is the cancellation. The emotion might be disappointment or hurt. But very quickly, thoughts begin forming around the event. One person might think, "They must be overwhelmed with something today." Another might think, "They don't value spending time with me." A third might conclude, "I always end up being the person people cancel on."

The difference between these interpretations can dramatically change the emotional experience that follows.

Thoughts can either soften emotions or intensify them. If the mind creates a story that frames the situation as temporary or understandable, the emotional reaction may remain manageable. If the story suggests rejection, failure, or threat, the emotional response can become far stronger.

After the thought comes behavior.

Behavior is the outward or inward action that follows the interpretation. It may involve words spoken during a conversation, a decision to withdraw, a defensive reaction, or even silent rumination. Behaviors are often the most visible part of the chain, which is why people tend to focus on them when trying to change.

Someone might say, "I need to stop overreacting," or "I should communicate better." But without understanding the earlier steps in the chain, behavioral change can feel extremely difficult. The reaction seems to appear automatically, leaving little time to choose a different response.

When the chain is understood clearly, something important becomes visible: the trigger is not the same as the story we attach to it.

Many emotional difficulties arise because the mind treats interpretation as if it were fact. The thought that appears in response to an event feels so convincing that it becomes indistinguishable from reality. If the mind concludes that a delayed message means rejection, the emotional system reacts as if rejection has already occurred.

Separating the event from the story creates space for a more balanced perspective.

Imagine again the message that says, "We need to talk later." The trigger is the message itself. The emotion might be uncertainty or concern. But the thought that follows could take many forms. If the mind automatically concludes that something is wrong, anxiety will grow. If the mind remains curious and open to multiple possibilities, the emotional reaction may stay calmer.

This distinction does not mean dismissing emotions or pretending that interpretations never matter. Instead, it allows you to recognize that emotions often arise before the full context of a situation is known.

Once this becomes clear, you can begin asking a powerful question during emotionally charged moments: what actually happened, and what story did my mind create about it?

The difference between those two elements can change the entire experience.

The trigger might be a comment from a supervisor during a meeting. The story might be that the comment proves you are not competent. The emotion might then become shame or anxiety. The behavior might involve withdrawing, overworking to compensate, or replaying the moment repeatedly in your mind.

But if the story shifts slightly, the emotional outcome can shift as well. The comment may still feel uncomfortable, but it may be interpreted as feedback rather than condemnation. The emotion might become determination instead of shame, leading to a different behavioral response.

This process does not happen perfectly or instantly. The mind's interpretations are shaped by long-standing emotional patterns, many of which developed years earlier. When those patterns are activated, the stories that appear can feel extremely convincing.

However, awareness of the chain weakens the automatic nature of those reactions. The moment you recognize that a story is forming, you regain some influence over how it develops.

Instead of reacting immediately, you can pause and examine the sequence. What was the trigger? What emotion appeared first? What interpretation followed? And what action am I about to take?

These questions do not eliminate emotions, but they transform confusion into understanding.

Over time, this practice builds emotional clarity. Situations that once felt overwhelming begin to reveal their internal structure. Instead of feeling lost inside reactions, you start recognizing the components that created them.

Clarity reduces emotional chaos. When the chain becomes visible, it becomes easier to intervene in it. You may not be able to control the trigger or stop an emotion from appearing, but you can learn to question the stories that intensify the reaction.

And that small shift can make a significant difference in how patterns evolve.

1.3 Mapping Your Patterns and What They Protect

Once you understand the chain connecting triggers, emotions, thoughts, and behaviors, the next step is to begin mapping how those elements appear in your life. Patterns often remain powerful because they operate in the background, repeating quietly without being examined closely. Bringing them into awareness transforms them from mysterious forces into understandable processes.

Pattern mapping is not about judging yourself or compiling a list of flaws. It is about learning how your emotional system has learned to respond to certain situations.

Every pattern contains information. It reveals where your emotional system feels threatened, where it seeks safety, and where it tries to protect you from pain.

Protection is an important concept here.

Many behaviors that appear self-defeating on the surface originally formed as protective strategies. Avoiding confrontation may have protected you from conflict in a volatile environment. Seeking constant approval may have helped you maintain connection in a household where attention was conditional. Emotional distance may have reduced vulnerability when closeness once led to disappointment.

These strategies made sense when they first developed. The challenge is that protective patterns often continue operating long after their original purpose has faded.

Mapping patterns allows you to see this clearly.

Start by reflecting on situations that repeatedly create strong emotional reactions. These moments may involve criticism, rejection, uncertainty, or conflict. They may also appear during moments that should feel positive, such as receiving attention, being offered opportunities, or forming deeper relationships.

For each situation, try to identify the elements of the emotional chain you explored earlier.

First consider the trigger. What happened externally that activated the reaction? Try to describe the event in simple terms without interpretation.

Next observe the emotion. What feeling appeared first? Was it fear, sadness, anger, embarrassment, or something more subtle like tension or unease?

After the emotion, examine the thoughts that followed. What conclusions did your mind reach about the situation? Did it assume rejection, failure, danger, or inadequacy?

Finally, consider the behavior that resulted. Did you withdraw, defend yourself, try to please others, or attempt to control the situation?

Writing these sequences down can reveal patterns that might otherwise remain hidden. You may notice that several different triggers lead to the same emotional reaction. You might see that similar thoughts appear across unrelated situations. Over time, these observations form a map of your emotional habits.

As the map develops, another question becomes important: what might this pattern be trying to protect?

At first this question may feel unusual. Many people assume their patterns exist only because something is wrong with them. But emotional systems are designed to prevent pain whenever possible. Even behaviors that create difficulties today may originally have served a protective role.

Consider someone who avoids difficult conversations. The behavior may frustrate them because it prevents honest communication. Yet the avoidance might be protecting them from a deeper fear of rejection or conflict. If past experiences taught them that disagreement leads to emotional distance, their mind may automatically steer away from situations that resemble that risk.

Another person might react strongly to criticism. The pattern may involve defensiveness or intense self-criticism. Beneath the surface, however, the reaction may be protecting a sense of worth that once felt fragile. If approval was inconsistent in the past, criticism may feel like confirmation of long-standing doubts.

Seeing patterns as protective responses changes the emotional tone of self-reflection. Instead of approaching yourself with frustration, you begin to approach your reactions with curiosity and compassion.

This perspective also prepares you for the deeper work ahead.

Patterns cannot change simply through willpower. They change when the emotional system learns that new responses are safe. By understanding what each pattern is trying to protect, you begin identifying the fears and needs that shaped it.

For example, if a pattern protects against rejection, the deeper need may be reassurance and connection. If it protects against conflict, the underlying need may be emotional safety. If it protects against failure, the core need may involve self-worth that is not dependent on performance.

These insights do not immediately eliminate the pattern, but they reveal the emotional terrain beneath it.

The reflective process introduced in this chapter serves as preparation for the next stage of the journey. Once you can see where your patterns appear most often and what they may be protecting, you will be ready to explore where those patterns began.

Every emotional habit has a history.

Understanding that history does not trap you in the past. Instead, it gives you the information necessary to reshape how your emotional system responds in the present.

For now, the task is simply to observe.

Notice the moments when reactions feel stronger than the situation seems to require. Pay attention to recurring fears, repeated relationship dynamics, and familiar internal criticisms. Each of these signals points toward a pattern that once helped you navigate the world.

By mapping these patterns with patience and honesty, you are already taking the first meaningful step toward changing them.

Chapter 2 — Understand Emotional Intelligence

2.1 The Skills That Shape Your Emotional World

Many people have heard the phrase *emotional intelligence*, yet surprisingly few understand what it truly means. The term is often used loosely in conversations about personal growth, leadership, and relationships. Some people assume it simply refers to being kind or patient. Others imagine it means staying calm all the time or avoiding conflict.

These interpretations miss the deeper reality.

Emotional intelligence is not about suppressing emotions, pretending everything is fine, or becoming endlessly agreeable. It is also not a personality trait that some people are born with while others are not. Emotional intelligence is a set of learnable skills that shape how you understand emotions, respond to them, and navigate relationships with others.

In practical terms, emotional intelligence answers several important questions. Can you recognize what you are feeling while it is happening? Can you pause before reacting when emotions become intense? Can you understand what someone else might be experiencing without immediately assuming their intentions? Can you communicate your needs clearly while still respecting the needs of others?

These abilities are not abstract concepts. They are everyday tools that influence the quality of your life.

Consider how often emotions influence decisions. A tense conversation can shape the direction of a relationship. A moment of discouragement can affect motivation at work. A feeling of insecurity can influence whether someone speaks up or stays silent. Emotions are constantly shaping behavior, yet many people move through life without learning how to work with them effectively.

This is where emotional intelligence becomes essential.

Rather than trying to eliminate emotions, emotional intelligence teaches you how to recognize them, understand their messages, and respond with intention rather than automatic reaction. It transforms emotions from unpredictable forces into sources of information.

To understand how this works, it helps to break emotional intelligence into five core abilities: self-awareness, self-regulation, empathy, motivation, and relationship skill.

These abilities are deeply connected. Each one strengthens the others, creating a balanced emotional system.

The first ability is self-awareness.

Self-awareness is the capacity to recognize what you are feeling as the emotion arises. It sounds simple, but in reality many people struggle with it. Emotions often appear quickly, and without awareness they blend together into a vague sense of tension or discomfort.

Someone might say they feel "stressed" when they are actually experiencing disappointment, fear, and frustration at the same time. Another person might feel irritated without recognizing that the irritation is covering sadness or hurt.

Self-awareness brings clarity to these experiences.

When you can identify what you are feeling, you gain the ability to respond more thoughtfully. Instead of reacting blindly, you begin to understand the emotional signals your mind and body are sending.

For example, recognizing anger may reveal that a boundary has been crossed. Recognizing sadness may highlight a need for connection or support. Recognizing anxiety may point toward uncertainty or fear that deserves attention.

Without self-awareness, emotions often control behavior. With awareness, they become information you can work with.

The second ability is self-regulation.

Self-regulation does not mean eliminating emotions or pretending they do not exist. It means managing emotional reactions so they do not overwhelm your ability to think clearly and act wisely.

Imagine feeling intense frustration during a disagreement. Without regulation, that frustration may lead to harsh words or defensive reactions that damage the relationship. With regulation, the emotion is still present, but you can pause long enough to respond thoughtfully.

Self-regulation involves skills such as slowing down reactions, calming the nervous system, and choosing responses that align with long-term values rather than momentary impulses.

Many people mistakenly believe that emotionally intelligent individuals never feel anger or frustration. In reality, emotionally intelligent people feel the same range of emotions as everyone else. The difference lies in how they handle those emotions.

Instead of being controlled by the reaction, they create space between the feeling and the action.

The third ability is empathy.

Empathy is the capacity to understand what another person may be feeling, even when their experience differs from your own. It involves recognizing emotional signals in tone, body language, and behavior.

Empathy does not require agreeing with someone or excusing harmful actions. It simply means acknowledging that another person's emotions exist and have meaning from their perspective.

In relationships, empathy acts as a bridge between people. When someone feels understood, defensiveness decreases and communication becomes easier. Without empathy, conversations can quickly turn into arguments where each person tries to prove their own viewpoint while ignoring the emotional experience of the other.

Empathy also helps prevent misunderstandings. When you consider what another person might be experiencing, you become less likely to assume negative intentions immediately.

For instance, if a colleague seems distant during a conversation, empathy encourages curiosity rather than judgment. Instead of assuming disinterest or disrespect, you may recognize that the person could be dealing with stress or distraction.

This shift in perspective can change the entire tone of an interaction.

The fourth ability is motivation.

In the context of emotional intelligence, motivation refers to the capacity to direct your energy toward meaningful goals despite emotional challenges.

Everyone experiences moments of discouragement, frustration, or doubt. These emotions can easily disrupt progress if they become overwhelming. Emotional intelligence helps maintain focus by connecting actions to deeper values and long-term aspirations.

Motivation is strengthened when people understand their emotional patterns. Instead of interpreting temporary setbacks as personal failures, emotionally intelligent individuals learn to view them as part of the learning process.

This ability to persist through difficulty is not based on relentless pressure or perfectionism. Instead, it comes from resilience—the capacity to recover from emotional setbacks and continue moving forward.

Motivation guided by emotional intelligence balances determination with self-compassion.

The fifth ability is relationship skill.

Human life is built around relationships. Whether at work, within families, or among friends, the ability to navigate interactions effectively plays a major role in well-being.

Relationship skill involves communicating clearly, resolving conflicts constructively, setting healthy boundaries, and maintaining mutual respect.

People with strong relationship skills understand that emotions influence every interaction. They pay attention not only to the words being spoken but also to the feelings underlying those words.

For example, during a disagreement they may notice rising tension and choose to slow the conversation down rather than escalate it. They may express concerns honestly while still acknowledging the perspective of the other person.

This balance allows difficult conversations to become opportunities for understanding rather than sources of damage.

Relationship skill is also closely connected to trust. When people feel emotionally understood and respected, trust grows naturally. When emotions are dismissed or ignored, relationships often become strained.

These five abilities—self-awareness, self-regulation, empathy, motivation, and relationship skill—work together to form the foundation of emotional intelligence.

None of them require perfection. They are abilities that grow through practice.

In fact, emotional intelligence often develops most effectively through everyday experiences. Each interaction becomes an opportunity to notice emotions, reflect on reactions, and experiment with new responses.

Over time, these small adjustments create meaningful change.

Instead of reacting impulsively, you begin responding with intention. Instead of misunderstanding others, you approach conversations with curiosity. Instead of feeling overwhelmed by emotions, you learn how to navigate them.

Perhaps the most important insight about emotional intelligence is that it is not about becoming emotionless. It is about becoming emotionally skilled.

Emotions are not obstacles to rational thinking. They are signals that help guide decisions, relationships, and personal growth. When those signals are understood clearly, they provide valuable guidance.

When they are ignored or misunderstood, they can create confusion and conflict.

The purpose of this chapter is to provide a functional model you can begin applying immediately. As you move through the rest of this book, you will return to these five abilities repeatedly.

Self-awareness will help you recognize patterns as they appear. Self-regulation will support healthier responses during challenging moments. Empathy will deepen your understanding of others. Motivation will sustain progress even when growth feels uncomfortable. Relationship skill will allow the changes within you to transform the connections around you.

Together, these abilities form the practical core of emotional intelligence.

They are not reserved for therapists, leaders, or experts. They are skills available to anyone willing to observe their emotional world with honesty and curiosity.

And once these skills begin to develop, they change the way you experience nearly every area of life.

2.2 Emotional Intelligence in Everyday Life

Understanding emotional intelligence conceptually is useful, but its true value appears when you see how it influences ordinary moments. Emotional skill does not operate only in dramatic situations or major life decisions. It shows itself in small choices that happen throughout the day. A conversation that could become an argument instead becomes a constructive exchange. A moment of disappointment becomes a lesson rather than a source of self-criticism. A stressful challenge becomes something that strengthens resilience rather than something that confirms self-doubt.

To understand the practical power of emotional intelligence, it helps to look at how it shapes four important areas of life: decision-making, conflict, resilience, and self-respect.

Decisions are rarely made through logic alone. Even when people believe they are acting rationally, emotions are quietly influencing the direction of their thinking. Fear can lead someone to avoid opportunities that might benefit them. Excitement can cause someone to overlook important risks. Shame can make a person stay silent when speaking up would protect their interests.

Emotional intelligence changes the relationship between feelings and choices.

Imagine someone offered a promotion that would require greater responsibility. Without emotional awareness, they might focus only on the anxiety that appears when thinking about the new role. That anxiety may lead them to decline the opportunity, even though it aligns with their long-term goals. From the outside, the decision might look like a simple preference for stability. Internally, however, it may have been driven by fear.

When emotional intelligence is present, the process looks different. The same anxiety may still arise, but instead of being treated as a command, it becomes a signal to explore. The person might ask themselves whether the fear reflects genuine risk or simply the discomfort that accompanies growth. By recognizing the emotional reaction without allowing it to dictate the decision, they gain greater freedom in how they respond.

This freedom does not mean ignoring emotions. It means understanding them well enough to prevent them from quietly controlling important choices.

Conflict provides another clear example of emotional intelligence in action. Disagreements are unavoidable in relationships, whether personal or professional. The difference between constructive conflict and damaging conflict often lies in how emotions are managed during the interaction.

Consider a situation in which two coworkers disagree about how to approach a project. Without emotional skill, the conversation may quickly shift from the issue itself to personal defensiveness. One person feels criticized and responds with frustration. The other feels misunderstood and raises their voice. Soon the discussion is no longer about the project but about protecting pride and proving who is right.

Emotional intelligence interrupts this escalation.

Someone with emotional awareness may notice the first signs of tension appearing in their body or tone of voice. Instead of reacting immediately, they pause long enough to acknowledge the emotion and refocus the conversation. They may say something as simple as, "I think we're both getting frustrated. Let's slow down and make sure we understand each other."

This response does not eliminate disagreement, but it changes the direction of the interaction. The conversation remains focused on solving the problem rather than defending identities.

Conflict handled with emotional intelligence often strengthens relationships instead of damaging them. When people feel heard and respected, even difficult conversations can build trust.

Resilience is another area where emotional intelligence becomes visible. Life inevitably brings setbacks: projects fail, relationships change, plans fall apart. Without emotional skill, these experiences can lead to harsh self-judgment or a sense of defeat.

Imagine someone who receives critical feedback after presenting an idea at work. Without emotional awareness, the feedback might trigger shame or embarrassment. The person may replay the moment repeatedly in their mind, interpreting the criticism as evidence that they are not capable or respected.

With emotional intelligence, the same feedback is experienced differently. The initial emotional reaction may still include disappointment or discomfort, but it does not define the entire experience. The person recognizes the emotion, allows it to pass, and then evaluates the feedback more objectively. They ask what can be learned from the situation rather than assuming it reflects their overall worth.

Resilience grows when people can experience emotional discomfort without being overwhelmed by it. Emotional intelligence provides the tools to navigate that discomfort.

Self-respect also emerges from emotional skill.

Many people struggle with boundaries because they feel responsible for maintaining harmony at all costs. They agree to requests they do not want to fulfill or remain silent when something feels unfair. Over time this pattern can create resentment and exhaustion.

Emotional intelligence supports a different approach.

Self-awareness helps individuals recognize when their needs are being ignored or dismissed. Self-regulation allows them to communicate those needs without reacting aggressively. Empathy enables them to consider the other person's perspective while still honoring their own limits.

For example, imagine someone who is repeatedly asked to take on extra responsibilities at work. Without emotional skill, they might accept the requests automatically, fearing that refusal would create tension or disapproval. Eventually they become overwhelmed and frustrated.

With emotional intelligence, the person notices the emotional signals that appear when another request arrives. Instead of suppressing those feelings, they interpret them as information. They respond calmly but clearly: "I want to help, but my schedule is already full. Let's talk about how we can prioritize the tasks."

This response maintains respect for both parties while protecting personal well-being.

Over time, decisions like these strengthen a sense of self-respect. The individual no longer feels trapped between pleasing others and protecting themselves. Emotional intelligence provides the balance that makes both possible.

These examples reveal an important truth: emotional intelligence does not remove difficulty from life. Challenges, disagreements, and uncertainty will always exist. What emotional skill changes is the way those challenges are experienced.

Instead of feeling controlled by reactions, you begin to navigate them with awareness. Instead of repeating the same conflicts, you approach them with curiosity and clarity. Instead of interpreting setbacks as personal failure, you treat them as opportunities for growth.

This shift creates a deeper form of personal freedom.

Freedom does not mean the absence of emotion. It means having the ability to respond to emotions rather than being ruled by them.

When emotional intelligence becomes part of daily life, the inner landscape becomes more stable. Decisions align more closely with values. Relationships become more authentic. Difficult moments still occur, but they no longer feel like proof that something is fundamentally wrong.

They become part of the process of learning and living.

2.3 Emotional Intelligence Is Built, Not Born

One of the most important truths about emotional intelligence is also one of the most encouraging. Emotional skill is not something reserved for a small group of naturally gifted people. It is not determined by personality, upbringing, or early life circumstances in a permanent way.

Emotional intelligence can be developed.

This idea may seem obvious, but many people carry a different belief beneath the surface. They assume that their emotional patterns are fixed. Someone might say, "I've always been bad at handling conflict," or "I'm just an anxious person." These statements sound like descriptions, but they often function as quiet conclusions about identity.

When people believe their emotional responses are permanent, growth feels impossible.

The truth is far more hopeful. Emotional intelligence develops through experience, reflection, and practice. The brain remains capable of learning new emotional responses throughout life.

Think of emotional intelligence as a set of muscles rather than a fixed trait. Muscles strengthen when they are used consistently. At first the effort may feel uncomfortable or awkward, but over time the body adapts and the ability grows.

Emotional skill follows a similar pattern.

Self-awareness improves when people practice observing their internal reactions. Self-regulation strengthens when they learn techniques for calming the nervous system during stress. Empathy grows when they become more attentive to the experiences of others. Motivation deepens when setbacks are approached as learning opportunities rather than personal failures. Relationship skills develop through honest communication and reflection.

None of these abilities appear instantly. They evolve gradually through repeated effort.

Understanding that emotional intelligence is learnable has another powerful effect: it replaces shame with possibility.

Many individuals feel embarrassed by their emotional reactions. They judge themselves harshly for feeling anxious, angry, or overwhelmed. This self-criticism often makes the situation worse because it adds another layer of tension to an already difficult moment.

When people realize that emotional intelligence can be developed, their perspective shifts. Instead of seeing emotional struggles as proof of weakness, they begin to see them as opportunities to learn.

A moment of frustration becomes a chance to practice self-regulation. A misunderstanding in a relationship becomes an opportunity to strengthen empathy and communication. A difficult emotion becomes a signal pointing toward something that deserves attention.

Growth replaces judgment.

This shift also brings direction to personal effort. Without a clear model of emotional intelligence, people often try to improve themselves through vague promises such as "I should be calmer" or "I need to be better at relationships." These goals are difficult to achieve because they lack specific skills.

Once emotional intelligence is understood as a combination of learnable abilities, improvement becomes more concrete. Instead of trying to change everything at once, people can focus on developing one skill at a time.

They might begin by practicing awareness of emotions during daily activities. Later they might experiment with new ways of responding to stress or communicating during conflict. Each small adjustment strengthens the overall system.

Over time, the emotional patterns that once felt automatic begin to shift.

This process is particularly important when working with deeper emotional wounds. Experiences from childhood or past relationships often leave strong impressions on the emotional system. These impressions may influence how people interpret situations, how safe they feel in close relationships, and how they evaluate their own worth.

Without emotional intelligence, these wounds can remain hidden yet powerful. They quietly shape behavior without being fully understood.

With emotional intelligence, however, those experiences can be explored with greater clarity and compassion. Self-awareness helps identify when an old emotional pattern is being activated. Self-regulation provides the stability needed to examine the feeling without becoming overwhelmed. Empathy allows individuals to treat their own past experiences with understanding rather than blame.

This combination creates the conditions for genuine healing.

Instead of trying to erase the past, people learn how to integrate it. They understand where certain reactions originated and gradually replace them with healthier responses.

This is why emotional intelligence is not only a tool for improving daily life but also a foundation for deeper emotional work.

The chapters ahead will explore how childhood experiences shape emotional patterns and how those patterns can be transformed. The skills introduced in this chapter will serve as guides throughout that process.

Self-awareness will help you recognize when old emotional memories are influencing present reactions. Self-regulation will allow you to stay grounded while examining those memories. Empathy will help you approach your younger self with compassion rather than criticism. Motivation will support persistence when the work feels challenging. Relationship skill will help translate internal healing into healthier connections with others.

By understanding that emotional intelligence can grow, you enter this journey with a different mindset. Instead of trying to prove your worth or fix something that feels broken, you approach the process as a form of learning.

And learning always carries the possibility of change.

The emotional patterns that once seemed permanent are not the final version of who you are. They are simply the starting point from which new skills and deeper understanding can emerge.

Chapter 3 — Meet Your Inner Child

3.1 The Voice From Earlier Years

At certain moments in life, people find themselves reacting in ways that seem strangely disproportionate to the situation in front of them. A brief disagreement might trigger deep hurt. A delayed message might cause a wave of anxiety. A small criticism might linger in the mind for days, replaying over and over as if it carried enormous weight.

When these reactions occur, the most common response is self-judgment. Many people tell themselves that they are being too sensitive, too emotional, or too dramatic. They try to silence the reaction quickly, hoping that if they ignore it long enough it will disappear.

But emotional reactions rarely disappear simply because they are criticized.

In many cases, these moments are not signs of weakness or immaturity. They are signals from parts of the emotional system that formed much earlier in life. They are echoes of experiences that shaped how safety, love, and belonging were understood long before adulthood began.

This is where the concept of the inner child becomes meaningful.

The inner child does not refer to childish behavior or an inability to grow up. Instead, it represents the emotional memory of earlier experiences—especially those that involved strong feelings, unmet needs, or moments of confusion and vulnerability.

Every person carries emotional impressions from childhood. These impressions are stored not only as memories but also as patterns of feeling and response. They influence how the mind interprets situations and how the body reacts to certain emotional signals.

Imagine a child who felt repeatedly ignored when trying to express sadness. Over time, that child may have learned that showing vulnerability does not bring comfort. Instead, it may lead to dismissal or embarrassment. As an adult, that person might struggle to express difficult emotions in relationships. They may withdraw during moments when support would actually help.

Another child might grow up in an environment where attention and affection were unpredictable. Some days were warm and reassuring, while others were distant or critical. In response, the child's emotional system learned to scan constantly for signs of rejection. As an adult, that heightened sensitivity may appear as anxiety about abandonment or a strong need for reassurance.

These responses were not created because the child was flawed. They were adaptive strategies designed to help the child navigate their environment.

Children are remarkably skilled at adjusting to the emotional conditions around them. When love feels uncertain, they learn to work harder for approval. When conflict feels threatening, they learn to stay quiet or become invisible. When expectations are extremely high, they may push themselves relentlessly in order to maintain connection.

At the time these strategies develop, they serve an important purpose. They protect the child from pain and increase the chances of maintaining attachment to caregivers.

The challenge appears when those same strategies continue operating long after the original environment has changed.

By adulthood, the individual may no longer need the same protective behaviors. Yet the emotional system still carries them as default responses. When certain situations resemble earlier experiences—even slightly—the inner child reacts as if the original conditions have returned.

This is why emotional triggers can feel confusing.

A person may know logically that their partner's brief distraction does not mean rejection, yet still feel a surge of fear when the partner becomes quiet. Another person may recognize that constructive feedback at work is normal, but still experience deep embarrassment or shame when hearing criticism.

These reactions are not irrational in the way people often assume. They are emotional memories resurfacing in response to familiar patterns.

The inner child is the part of the emotional system that remembers those patterns most strongly.

Understanding this perspective changes the way you relate to your own reactions. Instead of interpreting them as failures of character, you begin to see them as messages from earlier experiences that were never fully resolved.

For example, imagine someone who feels intense discomfort whenever conflict appears in a relationship. Their immediate impulse might be to apologize quickly or withdraw from the conversation. From the outside, this behavior might look like an inability to handle disagreement.

But if the person pauses to explore the reaction, they may discover that conflict once meant something very different in their childhood environment. Perhaps arguments between adults were loud, unpredictable, or emotionally painful. The child may have learned that disagreement threatened the sense of safety in the home.

As an adult, even mild disagreement may trigger the same emotional alarm system.

When viewed through this lens, the reaction becomes understandable rather than shameful.

The inner child is not trying to sabotage the present. It is attempting to prevent the repetition of earlier pain.

This realization introduces a profound shift in perspective. Instead of asking, "Why am I like this?" with frustration, you begin asking, "What part of me is trying to stay safe?"

That question opens the door to compassion.

Compassion does not mean excusing harmful behavior or avoiding responsibility for change. It means recognizing that many emotional responses began as attempts to cope with difficult circumstances.

Children do not have the freedom or resources that adults possess. They cannot easily change their environment or seek alternative support systems. Their emotional survival depends on adapting to the conditions around them.

Those adaptations become part of their internal world.

Over time, these patterns shape how individuals view themselves. A child who was frequently criticized may internalize the belief that they are never quite good enough. A child who had to manage the emotional needs of adults may grow up believing that their own needs are less important.

These beliefs often remain invisible because they feel familiar. They become quiet assumptions about how the world works.

The inner child carries these assumptions forward, influencing reactions long after the original events have faded into the background.

Meeting your inner child means becoming aware of these emotional echoes.

It involves noticing when a reaction feels unusually strong and asking whether the intensity might be connected to something earlier. It means recognizing that parts of your emotional system may still be responding to situations from the perspective of a younger self.

For many people, this realization brings relief.

Instead of seeing themselves as overly sensitive or emotionally flawed, they begin to understand that their reactions have history and meaning. The discomfort they feel is not random; it is connected to moments when their emotional needs were not fully met.

This understanding reduces self-judgment.

Imagine hearing a younger version of yourself expressing fear or sadness. Most people would respond with patience and reassurance rather than criticism. They would recognize that the child's feelings deserve attention and care.

The inner child invites that same response toward your own emotional experiences.

When a strong reaction appears, it may help to imagine that part of you as a younger voice seeking recognition. The emotion may represent a need that once went unheard: the need for comfort, safety, respect, or understanding.

Listening to that voice does not mean allowing it to control every decision. Instead, it means acknowledging its presence and responding with the wisdom and stability that adulthood provides.

This relationship between the adult self and the inner child becomes the foundation for emotional healing.

The adult self brings perspective, reasoning, and the ability to make choices. The inner child brings emotional truth, vulnerability, and the memory of what once felt painful or confusing.

When these two aspects begin working together, something powerful happens. Emotional reactions that once felt overwhelming become opportunities for understanding.

Instead of pushing feelings away, you become curious about what they represent. Instead of criticizing yourself for reacting strongly, you begin asking what the reaction might be protecting.

This approach transforms emotional growth from a battle against yourself into a conversation with yourself.

The goal is not to erase the inner child or silence its voice. The goal is to create a supportive relationship with that part of your emotional world.

As you continue through this chapter and the ones that follow, you will explore how early experiences shaped many of the patterns you identified earlier. You will learn how to recognize the moments when the inner child is influencing your reactions and how to respond with greater understanding.

For now, the most important step is simple recognition.

The emotional reactions that appear in your life today did not emerge from nowhere. They were shaped by experiences that mattered deeply at the time. The inner child carries the emotional memory of those experiences.

When you begin to meet that part of yourself with curiosity instead of judgment, the path toward healing becomes clearer.

3.2 When the Inner Child Appears in Adult Life

One of the reasons the inner child remains difficult to recognize is that it rarely appears in obvious ways. Most adults do not walk through life feeling like children. They have responsibilities, careers, relationships, and a long list of daily demands that require maturity and discipline. From the outside, their lives may look stable and capable.

Yet emotional patterns often reveal something deeper happening beneath the surface.

The inner child tends to show itself through behaviors that seem rational at first glance but carry a surprising amount of emotional intensity. These behaviors often develop as strategies for protection. They helped a younger version of the person manage uncertainty, avoid rejection, or maintain connection in environments where emotional needs were not consistently met.

Over time those strategies can become deeply ingrained habits.

Perfectionism is one of the most common examples. Many people describe perfectionism as a personality trait, something tied to ambition or high standards. But when examined more closely, perfectionism often carries an emotional message from earlier experiences.

Imagine a child growing up in an environment where praise appears mainly when achievements are impressive. The child quickly learns that approval and attention increase when performance is flawless. Mistakes, on the other hand, may lead to disappointment or criticism.

Without consciously realizing it, the child begins associating worth with performance.

As adulthood arrives, the habit remains. The person may feel constant pressure to do everything correctly, avoid mistakes, and maintain a polished image. They may struggle to relax because any error feels like evidence of failure.

From the outside, perfectionism might look like discipline. Inside, however, it often reflects a younger voice asking a silent question: *Will I still be valued if I am not perfect?*

People-pleasing follows a similar pattern.

A child raised in an emotionally unpredictable environment may learn that keeping others happy reduces tension. If caregivers were easily frustrated, overwhelmed, or distant, the child may have adapted by becoming highly attentive to other people's moods. They might learn to anticipate needs, agree quickly, or avoid expressing opinions that could create conflict.

This strategy may have helped preserve connection during childhood.

As an adult, the same pattern may appear as difficulty saying no, discomfort with disagreement, or a constant effort to meet everyone else's expectations. The person may feel responsible for maintaining harmony in every situation.

The behavior can appear generous or cooperative, but it often carries an emotional cost. When someone consistently prioritizes others' needs over their own, resentment and exhaustion tend to follow.

Underneath the pattern, the inner child may still be asking a quiet question: *If I stop pleasing others, will I still be accepted?*

Fear of rejection is another place where the inner child often appears.

Human beings are naturally wired for connection. Belonging is not simply a preference but a fundamental emotional need. When early experiences involve exclusion, criticism, or emotional distance, the mind becomes highly alert to signs that rejection might happen again.

As adults, individuals with this sensitivity may interpret ambiguous situations as potential rejection. A delayed response to a message may trigger anxiety. A partner's quiet mood may feel like emotional withdrawal. Even neutral feedback can sometimes be interpreted as disapproval.

These reactions are not signs of irrational thinking. They are protective mechanisms that once helped the child prepare for emotional pain.

The inner child learned that rejection was deeply uncomfortable, perhaps even threatening to the sense of belonging. As a result, the adult mind remains vigilant for similar signals.

Anger can also carry the voice of the inner child, though it often appears in ways that confuse people.

Some individuals struggle with frequent irritation or bursts of frustration that seem out of proportion to the situation. They may later regret their reactions and wonder why their emotions felt so overwhelming.

Anger, in many cases, is not the original emotion. It is a protective layer covering something more vulnerable underneath.

A child who felt powerless, unheard, or treated unfairly may have learned that anger was the only emotion that brought attention. Expressing sadness or fear may have been ignored or discouraged, while anger forced others to respond.

When that pattern carries into adulthood, anger may appear quickly in moments when the person feels dismissed, criticized, or misunderstood.

Beneath the anger, however, often lies a younger part that once felt hurt or invisible.

Emotional shutdown represents another protective strategy that can emerge from early experiences.

In environments where emotions were overwhelming or unsafe to express, children sometimes learn to disconnect from their feelings. Instead of reacting strongly, they become quiet, distant, or numb during difficult moments.

This response can be incredibly effective in protecting the child from emotional overload. If conflict, sadness, or chaos feel unbearable, shutting down may be the only available coping strategy.

As adults, individuals who developed this pattern may find themselves withdrawing during emotionally intense conversations. They may struggle to describe what they feel or feel uncomfortable when others express strong emotions.

Partners or friends might interpret the shutdown as indifference, when in reality it is a protective response learned long ago.

Recognizing these patterns is an important step in understanding the inner child.

Each of these behaviors—perfectionism, people-pleasing, fear of rejection, anger, and emotional shutdown—can be understood as attempts to maintain safety and connection. They were not created randomly. They were shaped by experiences that mattered deeply during earlier stages of life.

When you begin to see these patterns through this lens, something important changes.

Instead of criticizing yourself for reacting in certain ways, you begin asking where those reactions might have started. You start recognizing that parts of your emotional world developed during times when you had far less control over your environment.

This recognition does not mean abandoning responsibility for your actions. It simply means understanding the origins of behaviors that once seemed confusing.

And with understanding comes the possibility of change.

3.3 How Early Experiences Shape Beliefs About Love, Safety, and Worth

As the influence of the inner child becomes clearer, another layer of understanding begins to emerge. Early experiences do not only shape behaviors; they also shape beliefs about how the world works.

Children draw conclusions from their environments constantly. These conclusions form the foundation of their emotional worldview. Even when the child cannot express those ideas in words, the emotional system absorbs them deeply.

Over time, these conclusions become beliefs about safety, love, and personal worth.

Safety is one of the earliest emotional lessons a child learns. If caregivers respond consistently with warmth and reassurance, the child begins to associate relationships with stability. The world feels predictable enough to explore.

However, if the environment feels chaotic, unpredictable, or emotionally distant, the child's understanding of safety becomes more complicated. The mind may learn that security can disappear suddenly or that emotional closeness carries risk.

These early impressions often remain active long after childhood ends.

An adult who grew up in an unpredictable environment may feel uneasy when life becomes calm. Stability can feel unfamiliar, even uncomfortable. Without realizing it, the person may anticipate disruption or struggle to trust that positive experiences will last.

Love is another belief shaped by early relationships.

Children learn what love looks like through the behavior of those around them. If affection is consistent and unconditional, the child learns that love does not depend on perfection. Mistakes and disagreements become part of normal human interaction.

But if affection appears only when certain expectations are met, the child may conclude that love must be earned.

As an adult, this belief can create pressure to perform constantly in order to maintain connection. The person may feel responsible for proving their worth in relationships or may struggle to accept care without feeling obligated to repay it immediately.

Worth itself often develops through similar processes.

A child who receives encouragement and recognition for their individuality tends to develop a stable sense of self-value. They learn that their presence has meaning beyond achievements or external approval.

When recognition is inconsistent or critical, however, the child may internalize doubts about their value. They may begin measuring their worth through accomplishments, comparison with others, or the approval they receive.

These beliefs are rarely conscious. Most adults do not walk around thinking, *I must be perfect to be loved* or *my worth depends on what I achieve.* Yet the emotional system may behave as if these beliefs are true.

This is where the inner child continues seeking protection.

The younger parts of the self carry memories of moments when safety felt uncertain, love felt conditional, or worth felt fragile. When similar situations arise in adulthood, those parts activate protective strategies automatically.

A disagreement in a relationship may trigger fears about losing connection. A mistake at work may activate concerns about being seen as inadequate. Silence from a friend may stir old worries about abandonment.

These reactions are not random. They reflect the emotional conclusions drawn earlier in life.

Recognizing these connections does not mean blaming the past for every present difficulty. Instead, it helps illuminate the emotional roots of patterns that otherwise feel mysterious.

When people begin identifying the younger parts of themselves that still seek protection, self-understanding deepens significantly.

You may notice that certain reactions belong to a much earlier emotional age. A moment of insecurity might feel less like the response of a confident adult and more like the response of someone much younger, searching for reassurance.

Seeing this difference allows the adult self to step in with greater awareness.

Instead of ignoring the younger reaction or criticizing it, you begin acknowledging what it represents. You might recognize that a part of you is seeking safety, validation, or understanding that once felt uncertain.

This awareness prepares the ground for healing.

The chapters that follow will explore ways to respond to these younger parts with compassion and support. Healing does not require erasing the past or pretending those experiences never happened. It involves creating a new relationship with the emotional patterns that formed during those earlier years.

For now, the task is observation.

Notice the beliefs that appear during difficult moments. Pay attention to situations that trigger strong emotional responses. Ask yourself what younger need might be seeking protection in those moments.

The answers may not appear immediately, but the questions themselves begin opening the door to deeper understanding.

And that understanding is the first step toward meaningful change.

Chapter 4 — Trace the Original Wound

4.1 Where the Pattern Began

By the time people reach adulthood, many emotional reactions feel like permanent parts of their personality. Someone may believe they are simply anxious in relationships, naturally defensive when criticized, or habitually distant when emotions become intense. These tendencies appear so consistently that they seem woven into the fabric of identity.

Yet most emotional patterns did not begin as personality traits. They began as responses to experiences that left a strong impression on the developing emotional system.

In earlier chapters, you explored the idea that recurring reactions often reflect the voice of the inner child—the emotional memory of earlier needs, fears, and adaptive strategies. The next step is to look more closely at the kinds of experiences that often shape those patterns.

These experiences are sometimes referred to as emotional wounds.

The word "wound" does not imply dramatic or traumatic events in every case. Some emotional wounds arise from situations that were subtle but repeated over time. They may have involved misunderstandings, unmet needs, or environments where certain feelings were not acknowledged or supported.

Because these experiences often occurred gradually, people sometimes struggle to recognize them. They may say things like, "Nothing terrible happened in my childhood," while still noticing patterns of insecurity, self-criticism, or emotional distance in their adult lives.

Tracing the original wound helps bring clarity to these patterns. It gives language to feelings that may have remained vague for years.

One of the most common emotional wounds involves abandonment.

Abandonment does not only refer to physical absence. It can also occur emotionally. A child may feel abandoned when caregivers are frequently unavailable, distracted, or inconsistent in their presence. The child may experience moments when comfort was needed but did not arrive, or when attention seemed to disappear without explanation.

From a child's perspective, these experiences can feel deeply confusing. Young children naturally assume that the behavior of adults reflects something about themselves. If connection disappears unexpectedly, the child may conclude that they did something wrong or that they are somehow unworthy of attention.

Over time, these experiences can shape a powerful belief: the belief that connection is fragile and may disappear without warning.

As adults, individuals who carry abandonment wounds often become highly sensitive to signs of distance in relationships. A delayed response to a message, a change in tone, or a temporary disagreement may trigger anxiety about losing connection. The emotional system remains alert for signals that closeness might vanish again.

Another common wound emerges through repeated criticism.

All children receive correction and guidance at times. Healthy feedback helps them learn and grow. But when criticism becomes constant, harsh, or emotionally charged, it can shape a child's sense of self in a very different way.

Imagine a child who hears frequent comments suggesting that their efforts are never quite good enough. Even if the intention behind those comments was to encourage improvement, the emotional message may be interpreted differently.

The child may begin to believe that approval must be earned through flawless performance.

Over time, this belief can lead to strong self-criticism. The adult may push themselves relentlessly, fearing that mistakes will reveal something fundamentally wrong with them. Even small errors may trigger embarrassment or shame.

Perfectionism often grows from this kind of wound. The person becomes driven to prove their worth through achievement, hoping that success will finally silence the internal voice of criticism.

Neglect forms another powerful emotional wound, though it often receives less attention because it can be subtle.

Neglect occurs when a child's emotional needs are consistently overlooked or minimized. Caregivers may provide food, shelter, and practical support while remaining emotionally distant or unavailable.

In these environments, the child may learn that feelings are inconvenient or unimportant. When sadness, fear, or excitement appear, there may be no one who responds with curiosity or empathy.

As a result, the child may begin suppressing emotional expression altogether.

The adult who grows from this environment may struggle to identify or communicate feelings. They may feel disconnected from their emotional world or uncomfortable when others express strong emotions. Relationships may remain surface-level because deeper emotional exchange feels unfamiliar.

Despite these patterns, the person may not immediately recognize neglect as a wound because basic physical needs were met. Yet emotional nourishment is just as important for development as physical care.

Another pattern appears in experiences of enmeshment.

Enmeshment occurs when boundaries between a child and caregiver become blurred. Instead of allowing the child to develop independence and personal identity, the relationship becomes overly intertwined. The child may feel responsible for the emotional well-being of the adult.

For example, a parent may share worries, frustrations, or personal problems in ways that place emotional pressure on the child. The child may become the listener, comforter, or mediator within the household.

At first glance, this dynamic may appear close or supportive. But the emotional roles are reversed. The child begins managing responsibilities that belong to the adult.

Over time, the child may internalize the belief that their value comes from caring for others. They may grow into adults who struggle to recognize their own needs because they are accustomed to focusing on everyone else's emotions first.

People-pleasing and difficulty setting boundaries often grow from this experience.

Inconsistent love forms another wound that shapes emotional patterns.

Children depend on predictable signals of affection and support to develop a stable sense of belonging. When warmth and approval appear unpredictably—sometimes present, sometimes withdrawn—the child's emotional system becomes uncertain about what to expect.

One day a caregiver may be affectionate and attentive. Another day they may be distant or critical. The child may try repeatedly to figure out what behavior leads to approval and what leads to withdrawal.

This uncertainty can create a constant search for reassurance.

As adults, individuals who experienced inconsistent love may feel anxious about whether they are truly valued in relationships. They may seek frequent confirmation that everything is still okay. They may also feel intense relief when receiving attention, followed by renewed worry when that attention fades.

The emotional system learned early that connection could change quickly, so it remains watchful for signs of change.

These wounds—abandonment, criticism, neglect, enmeshment, and inconsistent love—do not exist as isolated categories. Many people experience more than one of them in varying degrees. The specific combination shapes the coping mechanisms that develop later.

Coping mechanisms are the strategies the emotional system uses to manage pain or uncertainty.

A person who experienced abandonment may become highly attentive to others' moods in order to preserve connection. Someone shaped by criticism may become driven by achievement in order to avoid judgment. Someone who experienced neglect may distance themselves emotionally because expressing needs once felt pointless.

At the time these strategies formed, they served an important purpose. They helped the child adapt to circumstances that were beyond their control.

But as life continues, the strategies can become limiting.

The adult who constantly anticipates rejection may struggle to trust stable relationships. The person driven by perfectionism may feel exhausted by relentless self-pressure. The individual who learned to suppress emotions may feel disconnected from their own inner life.

Tracing the original wound helps explain why these patterns exist.

Instead of interpreting them as random flaws, you begin to see them as intelligent responses to earlier conditions. The emotional system did not create these habits without reason. It was trying to maintain safety, connection, or belonging in the only ways available at the time.

Language plays an important role in this process.

Many people have lived for years with emotional discomfort they cannot easily describe. They may feel persistent insecurity or distance without knowing why. When the experiences behind those feelings are named, the confusion often begins to soften.

A person who has struggled with perfectionism for years may suddenly recognize how closely it relates to earlier criticism. Someone who has always feared rejection may begin connecting that fear to moments of emotional absence in childhood.

This recognition does not change the past, but it transforms how the present is understood.

Instead of seeing emotional patterns as mysterious forces, you begin to see their origins.

Tracing the wound is not about assigning blame to caregivers or dwelling on painful memories. Many parents and caregivers did the best they could with the resources and knowledge available to them. Emotional wounds often emerge from ordinary circumstances where certain needs were unintentionally overlooked.

The purpose of this exploration is understanding.

When you understand where a pattern began, you gain the ability to respond to it differently. The adult self can begin recognizing when an old coping mechanism is being activated and gently question whether it is still necessary.

This awareness prepares the ground for healing.

In the chapters ahead, you will explore how emotional intelligence can be used to respond to these wounds with compassion and intention. The coping strategies that once felt automatic can gradually be replaced with healthier responses that support both connection and self-respect.

For now, the task is simply recognition.

Many emotional reactions that once felt confusing begin to make sense when viewed through the lens of earlier experiences. The patterns you carry today may have started long ago, but they are not permanent definitions of who you are.

They are the starting points from which healing can begin.

4.2 How Family Systems Shape Emotional Survival

To understand emotional wounds fully, it is not enough to look at isolated events. Human development takes place within systems—families, households, schools, and communities that each carry their own emotional climate. These environments shape how children learn to interpret feelings, how they respond to conflict, and what strategies they use to maintain connection with others.

Children do not simply observe these environments from a distance. They absorb them. Every interaction, tone of voice, and emotional reaction becomes part of an ongoing lesson about how relationships work.

In many cases, the strategies children develop are remarkably intelligent. They are attempts to maintain safety, stability, or belonging in circumstances that might otherwise feel overwhelming. When viewed through the lens of adulthood, these strategies sometimes appear self-defeating. But when viewed from the perspective of a child navigating their environment, they often make perfect sense.

Family systems play a central role in this process.

Every family develops its own emotional patterns. Some families communicate openly and encourage emotional expression. Others avoid difficult conversations entirely. Some emphasize independence, while others expect strong loyalty and closeness among members.

Children adapt to these patterns automatically. They learn how emotions are handled within the system and adjust their behavior accordingly.

For example, in a household where conflict is frequent and unpredictable, a child may become highly alert to changes in mood or tone. They might learn to read subtle signals in order to anticipate arguments before they escalate. This sensitivity helps the child prepare emotionally or attempt to reduce tension.

As adults, individuals who developed this awareness may continue scanning environments for signs of conflict. They may feel uneasy in situations where others seem calm but small emotional shifts occur. Their mind has been trained to notice signals others might overlook.

In another family environment, emotions might rarely be discussed at all. Difficult feelings could be dismissed quickly with statements such as "Don't worry about it" or "Just move on." In these systems, children may learn that emotional expression is unnecessary or inconvenient.

The child adapts by minimizing their own feelings. They may focus on practical tasks, achievements, or responsibilities instead of emotional experiences. This strategy helps them function within the environment they know.

As adults, however, these individuals may find it difficult to identify what they are feeling or communicate emotional needs.

What once helped them fit into their family system now creates distance in relationships where emotional openness is important.

Caregivers also influence emotional development through their own coping patterns.

Parents and guardians carry their own histories, stresses, and emotional habits. Some caregivers may have grown up in environments where emotions were ignored or criticized. Others may have experienced hardship that shaped their reactions to stress.

Children often internalize these patterns without realizing it.

If a caregiver reacts to frustration with anger, the child may learn that anger is the primary way to express distress. If a caregiver withdraws during difficult conversations, the child may learn that emotional distance is the safest response to tension.

These lessons do not occur through formal instruction. They develop through observation and repetition.

Over time, the child constructs a set of emotional survival strategies designed to maintain connection with caregivers and navigate the emotional environment of the household.

Some children respond by becoming highly responsible and mature at an early age. They take care of tasks, help resolve conflicts, or attempt to support the emotional needs of adults. This pattern can lead to strong competence and reliability later in life, but it may also create difficulty asking for help or expressing vulnerability.

Other children respond by becoming highly agreeable. They learn to avoid disagreement or criticism in order to keep relationships stable. This strategy can make them attentive and cooperative adults, yet it may also lead to people-pleasing and difficulty asserting boundaries.

Still others adapt by becoming independent and emotionally self-reliant. If emotional support was rarely available, the child may learn to rely entirely on themselves. As adults, they may appear strong and capable but struggle with closeness or trust.

Each of these patterns reflects a form of intelligence.

The child's emotional system is constantly searching for ways to preserve connection and reduce distress. Even when the environment is imperfect or unpredictable, the mind attempts to find strategies that allow the child to cope.

Understanding this process changes the way many people view their own struggles.

Instead of seeing patterns as evidence of personal failure, they begin recognizing the creativity and resilience that shaped those responses. The strategies that now feel limiting once served an important purpose.

This perspective reduces self-blame.

For many individuals, learning about emotional survival strategies brings a sense of relief. They realize that the behaviors they have criticized themselves for were not random flaws. They were attempts to survive emotionally complex environments.

At the same time, understanding these patterns does not remove personal responsibility.

Adults still have the ability—and the responsibility—to examine their habits and decide whether those strategies continue serving their lives in healthy ways. What once helped maintain safety in childhood may no longer be necessary in adulthood.

The goal is not to erase these strategies entirely but to update them.

Emotional growth involves recognizing when an old pattern is operating and deciding whether a new response might be more helpful in the present moment. This balance allows individuals to appreciate the resilience that shaped them while still pursuing change.

Through this process, the past becomes a source of insight rather than a fixed limitation.

Chapter 5 — Build Emotional Safety

5.1 Why Safety Comes Before Healing

When people begin exploring their emotional history, a natural impulse often appears. They want answers quickly. Once they realize that childhood experiences may have shaped many of their current patterns, it can feel urgent to uncover every memory, every wound, and every explanation as fast as possible.

The desire is understandable. When something in life has caused confusion or pain for years, clarity feels like relief waiting just beneath the surface. Many people assume that the faster they reach the root of the problem, the faster they will be able to fix it.

Yet emotional healing does not work in the same way that solving a technical problem does.

Insight alone rarely creates lasting change. In fact, when people attempt to examine painful experiences too quickly or too intensely, the process can become overwhelming. Instead of leading to clarity, it can trigger emotional flooding that makes reflection almost impossible.

This is why emotional safety must come first.

Emotional safety means creating conditions in which the mind and body feel stable enough to explore difficult experiences without becoming overwhelmed by them. It does not mean avoiding emotions or pretending that painful memories do not exist. Rather, it means approaching those memories in a way that the nervous system can tolerate and integrate.

Understanding the role of the nervous system is essential here.

Human beings are equipped with a biological system designed to detect and respond to threats. When danger appears, the body activates protective responses that prepare us to fight, flee, or shut down. These reactions occur automatically and often faster than conscious thought.

In situations involving physical danger, this system is extremely helpful. It increases alertness, mobilizes energy, and focuses attention on survival.

However, the same system also responds to emotional threats.

Experiences that resemble earlier moments of rejection, criticism, abandonment, or helplessness can activate the same protective responses. The body may react with tension, racing thoughts, rapid breathing, or a strong urge to escape the situation.

When the nervous system enters this state of overwhelm, the brain's ability to reflect and learn becomes limited. The parts of the brain responsible for careful reasoning and emotional understanding temporarily step back while survival responses take the lead.

In this state, insight is difficult to access.

Someone might attempt to analyze a painful memory but find themselves flooded with emotion. Another person might suddenly feel numb or detached while discussing certain experiences. Others may become restless, anxious, or unable to concentrate.

These reactions are not signs that healing is failing. They are signals that the nervous system has moved beyond the range where learning and integration are possible.

Emotional safety keeps the nervous system within a range where reflection can occur.

Think of this range as a window of tolerance. Within this window, emotions can be felt without becoming overwhelming. The mind remains capable of curiosity and perspective. Outside of this window, emotional intensity becomes either too strong or too muted for meaningful processing.

When emotions are too intense, people may experience panic, anger, or deep distress. When emotions become too muted, they may feel numb, disconnected, or distant from their experiences.

Healing work happens most effectively within the middle range.

Building emotional safety helps expand and stabilize that range.

One important aspect of emotional safety is pacing. Many people initially resist the idea of slowing down. They worry that moving gradually means avoiding the real work or delaying progress.

In reality, pacing is part of progress.

When emotional exploration happens at a pace the nervous system can handle, new insights are more likely to integrate into everyday life. The mind has time to reflect, absorb information, and adjust patterns gradually.

Attempting to force rapid breakthroughs often leads to cycles of emotional overwhelm followed by withdrawal. The individual may explore painful memories intensely for a short period, then feel exhausted or discouraged afterward. Eventually they may avoid the process altogether.

Pacing prevents this cycle.

It allows emotional understanding to grow in layers rather than bursts. Each step builds stability before moving deeper into more complex material.

Another element of emotional safety involves recognizing the difference between exploration and re-experiencing.

Exploration means examining past experiences with awareness and perspective. The adult self remains present and capable of observing the memory.

Re-experiencing occurs when the emotional intensity of the past feels as if it is happening again in the present. In this state, the nervous system reacts as though the earlier situation has returned.

Healing requires exploration rather than re-experiencing.

The adult self must remain anchored in the present moment while reflecting on earlier experiences. This anchoring helps remind the nervous system that the conditions are different now. The person has resources, understanding, and support that may not have been available in the past.

Emotional safety strengthens this sense of stability.

Supportive environments play an important role as well. Healing rarely happens in isolation from the world around us. The relationships, routines, and spaces we inhabit influence how safe we feel while exploring difficult emotions.

For some people, emotional safety grows through conversations with trusted friends or therapists who provide understanding without judgment. For others, it develops through personal practices such as journaling, meditation, or reflective walks in quiet environments.

What matters most is the presence of conditions that allow emotional experiences to unfold without pressure or criticism.

Self-compassion is another key ingredient.

When people begin examining emotional wounds, they sometimes react with harsh self-judgment. They may feel embarrassed about their reactions or frustrated that certain patterns still exist in their lives.

These responses often make emotional exploration more difficult.

Self-compassion changes the tone of the process. Instead of approaching emotional reactions as problems that need to be eliminated immediately, individuals learn to treat them as signals worth understanding.

This shift does not mean ignoring responsibility for change. It simply replaces harsh criticism with curiosity and care.

Imagine speaking to a younger version of yourself who experienced confusion, fear, or sadness. Most people would not respond with blame or impatience. They would offer reassurance and understanding.

Emotional safety involves extending that same attitude toward your own internal experiences.

As this approach develops, something important begins to happen. The nervous system gradually learns that emotional exploration does not automatically lead to overwhelm. It becomes possible to approach memories and patterns with increasing stability.

This stability creates the conditions necessary for deeper healing.

Without emotional safety, insight often remains intellectual. A person might understand where a pattern came from but still feel powerless to change it because the emotional reactions remain too strong.

With emotional safety, the mind and body can begin integrating new responses. Old patterns become less automatic because the nervous system is no longer locked in protective modes.

It is also important to recognize that emotional safety is not a final destination reached once and for all. It is something that grows through repeated experiences of stability and care.

Some days may feel easier than others. Certain memories may require slower exploration than expected. These variations are normal.

Progress in emotional healing is rarely linear. It often moves forward through cycles of insight, reflection, and adjustment.

Pacing allows these cycles to unfold naturally.

When people learn to respect the rhythm of their emotional system, they discover that slowing down often leads to deeper change than rushing forward. What initially feels like patience eventually reveals itself as wisdom.

The purpose of this chapter is to establish a foundation for the work ahead. The next stages of healing will involve reconnecting with earlier experiences and learning new ways to respond to them.

But before those steps can be taken safely, the emotional system must feel supported and stable.

Building emotional safety is not a detour from healing. It is the ground on which healing stands.

When the nervous system feels secure enough to remain present with difficult emotions, the mind becomes capable of understanding and transformation. And from that place of stability, real change can begin to unfold.

5.2 Creating Inner Stability Through Grounding and Emotional Regulation

Once the importance of emotional safety is understood, the next step is learning how to create that safety within yourself. Many people begin exploring emotional wounds with good intentions but quickly discover that strong feelings can appear unexpectedly. A memory may surface, a difficult realization may emerge, or a conversation may trigger emotions that feel larger than anticipated.

Without tools to stay present during these moments, the natural tendency is to escape the feeling or shut it down. Some people distract themselves immediately through work, technology, or constant activity. Others mentally analyze the experience without allowing themselves to feel it. Still others collapse into the emotion so completely that they feel overwhelmed and powerless.

Neither extreme supports healing.

Avoiding emotions prevents insight, while drowning in them prevents reflection. Emotional healing requires a middle ground where feelings can be experienced without taking control of the entire system. This is where grounding, self-soothing, and emotional check-ins become essential.

Grounding is the practice of reconnecting your attention to the present moment, especially when your mind begins drifting toward distressing memories, worries about the future, or intense emotional reactions. It helps remind the nervous system that you are here, now, and safe enough to remain aware.

One of the reasons grounding works is because emotional overwhelm often pulls attention away from the present. When strong emotions appear, the mind may replay past experiences or imagine catastrophic outcomes. The body may respond as if danger is immediate, even when the current environment is stable.

Grounding gently interrupts that process.

The simplest form of grounding involves shifting attention to physical sensations. Feeling your feet against the floor, noticing the rhythm of your breathing, or paying attention to the sensations in your hands can bring awareness back to the body. These small moments of attention send signals to the nervous system that the present moment is different from the past event being remembered.

Another aspect of grounding involves orienting yourself to your surroundings. Looking around the room, noticing colors, shapes, or sounds, and reminding yourself where you are can help anchor the mind in current reality. These simple observations activate parts of the brain associated with awareness and orientation, helping counterbalance emotional flooding.

Grounding does not erase emotions, nor is it meant to suppress them. Instead, it creates enough stability that emotions can be felt without overwhelming the system.

Self-soothing practices serve a similar purpose but focus more directly on calming the nervous system.

When emotional reactions intensify, the body often enters a state of heightened activation. The heart rate may increase, breathing may become shallow, and muscles may tighten. These physical changes prepare the body for action but make reflection more difficult.

Self-soothing techniques help bring the body back toward a calmer state.

Slow breathing is one of the most effective methods. Taking slow, steady breaths and extending the exhale slightly longer than the inhale can signal the nervous system to reduce its level of alertness. This shift allows the body to move away from a state of threat and toward one of stability.

Gentle physical movements can also help. Stretching, walking slowly, or placing a hand over your heart or stomach can create a sense of connection with the body. These small gestures remind the emotional system that care and attention are present.

Some people find comfort in sensory experiences such as warm tea, soft lighting, calming music, or familiar scents. These sensations may seem simple, but they help regulate the nervous system by providing signals of safety and familiarity.

The purpose of self-soothing is not to avoid emotions but to support yourself while experiencing them.

When the nervous system feels supported, it becomes easier to stay with difficult feelings long enough to understand them. This creates trust in the healing process because the individual learns that emotional intensity can rise and fall without causing permanent distress.

Emotional check-ins add another layer to this process.

Many people move through their day with limited awareness of their internal emotional state. They may notice stress or discomfort only when it becomes intense. Emotional check-ins create small moments of awareness that prevent feelings from building unnoticed.

An emotional check-in is simply a pause to ask yourself what you are feeling in the present moment. This question can be surprisingly powerful.

You might notice tension in your body, fatigue from the day's demands, or subtle anxiety about an upcoming conversation. Instead of ignoring these signals, the check-in acknowledges them. This awareness allows you to respond with care before the emotion becomes overwhelming.

Regular check-ins also help develop emotional vocabulary. Instead of labeling everything as stress or frustration, you may begin distinguishing between disappointment, worry, sadness, irritation, or loneliness. Each emotion carries different information about what you may need.

Over time, emotional check-ins strengthen self-awareness and self-regulation simultaneously. The more familiar you become with your internal signals, the easier it becomes to respond to them with balance.

Together, grounding, self-soothing, and emotional check-ins create a sense of internal stability. They help you remain present during emotional exploration instead of escaping into distraction or collapsing into overwhelm.

This stability builds trust.

When people experience that they can feel difficult emotions and still remain grounded, their confidence in the healing process grows. They begin to understand that emotions are temporary waves rather than permanent storms.

With practice, these tools become reliable companions during emotional work. They allow insight to unfold gradually while maintaining connection to the present moment.

Chapter 6 — Reparent With Compassion

6.1 Becoming the Support You Once Needed

As people begin understanding their emotional patterns, a powerful realization often emerges. Many of the reactions that appear in adult life were shaped during periods when emotional support, guidance, or validation may have been incomplete. Earlier chapters explored how wounds can form when needs for safety, attention, understanding, or stability are not consistently met.

Recognizing these patterns is an important step, but recognition alone does not complete the healing process.

Understanding where pain began can explain why certain reactions exist, yet the emotional system still carries the original need beneath the pattern. A child who felt unseen still longs to be recognized. A child who was frequently criticized still seeks reassurance that mistakes do not erase their worth. A child who felt alone during difficult moments still searches for a sense of protection and care.

Healing happens when those needs begin to receive new responses.

This is where the principle of reparenting becomes central.

Reparenting means learning to provide for yourself the emotional qualities that may have been missing earlier in life. These qualities include validation, protection, encouragement, guidance, and compassion. Instead of continuing to search for these experiences only from others, you begin cultivating them internally.

At first this idea can feel unfamiliar. Many people are accustomed to thinking of care as something that comes primarily from outside sources—parents, partners, friends, or mentors. While supportive relationships remain valuable throughout life, emotional growth also requires the development of an internal relationship with oneself.

Reparenting is the process of strengthening that relationship.

It involves becoming the kind of inner authority who responds to emotional experiences with steadiness rather than criticism. When painful memories or strong reactions appear, the goal is no longer simply to analyze them. The goal becomes responding to those moments with the care and clarity that may have been absent before.

To understand why this approach matters, it helps to consider how inner dialogue develops.

Many people carry internal voices that sound remarkably similar to messages they heard growing up. A person who experienced frequent criticism may have an internal voice that quickly points out mistakes. Someone raised in an environment where emotions were dismissed may find themselves minimizing their own feelings automatically.

These internal voices operate quietly but powerfully. They shape how individuals interpret events and how they respond to themselves during moments of difficulty.

Reparenting introduces a different voice into this internal conversation.

Instead of responding to emotional pain with harsh judgment, the adult self begins responding with curiosity and support. Instead of saying, "You shouldn't feel this way," the inner dialogue shifts toward understanding: "Something here matters. Let's slow down and listen."

This change may seem small, but it alters the entire emotional landscape.

Imagine a child who falls and scrapes their knee. One caregiver might react by dismissing the pain and telling the child to stop crying. Another might kneel beside the child, acknowledge the hurt, and offer reassurance. The physical injury is the same in both situations, yet the emotional experience becomes very different depending on the response.

The same principle applies internally.

When emotional pain appears and the internal response is criticism or dismissal, the wound deepens. When the response is compassionate attention, the nervous system begins to relax.

Reparenting is essentially the practice of becoming the second caregiver in that example.

You begin responding to your own emotional experiences with presence rather than impatience. This response sends an important message to the nervous system: you are not alone in this moment.

One of the first elements of reparenting is validation.

Validation means acknowledging that your emotional reactions make sense in the context of your experiences. It does not mean agreeing with every impulse or behavior. Instead, it recognizes that emotions arise for reasons that deserve attention.

For instance, if you notice anxiety when someone seems distant, validation might sound like this: "It makes sense that this feels uncomfortable. Earlier experiences taught me that distance can signal rejection." This response does not automatically assume the worst about the current situation, but it acknowledges the emotional history involved.

Validation helps reduce the internal conflict that occurs when feelings are criticized or denied.

Another element of reparenting involves protection.

Children rely on caregivers to create boundaries and provide a sense of safety. When those boundaries were unclear or inconsistent, the child may have felt responsible for managing situations beyond their control.

As adults, individuals sometimes continue tolerating environments or relationships that create emotional distress because they never learned how to protect their own well-being.

Reparenting introduces a new role for the adult self: the role of protector.

This means recognizing when situations violate personal values or emotional limits and responding with appropriate boundaries. Protection does not require aggression or withdrawal. It simply means acknowledging that your needs and emotional safety matter.

Encouragement also plays an important role.

Children develop confidence when caregivers recognize effort and progress. When encouragement is missing or overshadowed by criticism, individuals may grow up doubting their abilities even when they perform well.

Reparenting replaces the constant pressure to be perfect with steady encouragement for growth.

This encouragement acknowledges that mistakes are part of learning rather than proof of failure. The adult self becomes a guide who supports progress rather than demanding impossible standards.

Guidance is another essential component.

Children often rely on caregivers to help them interpret experiences and make decisions. Without guidance, situations that involve uncertainty or challenge can feel overwhelming.

Reparenting provides an internal source of direction. Instead of reacting impulsively or relying entirely on external approval, the adult self begins asking thoughtful questions about what choices align with personal values and well-being.

Guidance brings clarity where confusion once existed.

Compassion ties all these elements together.

Compassion means approaching your emotional world with patience rather than impatience. It recognizes that healing takes time and that setbacks are natural parts of the process.

Many people initially struggle with self-compassion because they believe it will lead to complacency or weakness. In reality, compassion often strengthens resilience. When individuals treat themselves with understanding during difficult moments, they recover more quickly and remain open to learning.

Reparenting transforms healing from passive reflection into an active relationship with yourself.

Instead of waiting for insights to appear or for others to provide reassurance, you begin participating directly in your own emotional growth. The adult self becomes an ally rather than an observer.

This shift creates a new kind of inner authority.

Authority in this context does not mean strict control or rigid rules. It refers to a steady presence that can hold emotions without becoming overwhelmed by them. The adult self becomes capable of acknowledging the inner child's feelings while also providing perspective and direction.

When anxiety appears, the inner authority does not dismiss it. Instead, it responds with reassurance and practical support. When anger arises, the authority listens to what boundary may have been crossed while guiding the response toward constructive action.

Over time, this relationship between the adult self and the inner child becomes more balanced.

The inner child continues expressing emotional truths, but it no longer carries the responsibility of navigating the world alone. The adult self provides the stability, protection, and understanding that were once uncertain.

This partnership forms the foundation of emotional repair.

Reparenting does not erase the past or eliminate every emotional reaction. Instead, it changes how those reactions are met. Moments that once triggered self-criticism now invite compassion. Situations that once created confusion now encourage reflection.

Healing becomes less about fixing something broken and more about strengthening a relationship that supports growth.

As this chapter continues, you will explore practical ways to practice reparenting in everyday life. These practices will help you respond to emotional experiences with the care and guidance that allow deeper healing to unfold.

For now, the most important shift is recognizing that the support you once needed does not have to remain absent. Through conscious awareness and compassionate practice, you can begin offering that support to yourself.

6.2 Practicing Compassion in Everyday Moments

Understanding the idea of reparenting can feel meaningful, but the real transformation happens when the concept becomes part of daily experience. Compassion toward yourself is not built through a single insight. It grows through repeated moments in which you respond to your emotions in a new way.

For many people, this is unfamiliar territory. They may have spent years responding to mistakes, fears, or disappointments with criticism or pressure. The inner voice that developed during those years often feels automatic. When something goes wrong, the mind quickly generates statements such as "You should have known better," or "Why can't you get this right?"

Reparenting begins when you recognize that voice and introduce a different one.

Compassionate self-talk is often the first step. Self-talk refers to the quiet commentary that runs through the mind throughout the day. Most people are not fully aware of how frequently it appears or how strongly it influences emotional states.

When the inner voice is harsh or dismissive, the emotional system remains tense. The body prepares for judgment rather than growth. Compassionate self-talk shifts that tone.

Instead of reacting to difficulty with criticism, the internal response begins to resemble what a supportive caregiver might say to a struggling child. If you feel anxious about a challenge, the compassionate voice might say, "This is difficult, and it makes sense that you feel nervous. Let's take it one step at a time."

If you make a mistake, the response might be, "Everyone makes errors while learning. What can I understand from this experience?"

These statements do not ignore responsibility. They simply remove unnecessary shame from the process of growth.

Over time, compassionate self-talk begins to reshape the emotional climate inside the mind. Instead of anticipating criticism, the inner child begins to experience understanding.

Another important practice involves identifying emotional needs.

One reason emotional reactions become intense is that the underlying need has remained unrecognized for years. A person might feel irritation during a conversation, but the deeper experience may involve feeling unheard or unimportant. Another person may feel sudden sadness without realizing that the emotion reflects a need for connection.

Needs identification involves pausing long enough to ask a simple question: what is this feeling asking for?

Sometimes the answer is straightforward. Fatigue may signal the need for rest. Loneliness may point toward a need for companionship or understanding. Anxiety may reflect the need for reassurance or clarity about an uncertain situation.

Other times the answer requires reflection. Emotional hunger may show up as the urge to seek constant validation or approval. Beneath that urge may be a deeper need for recognition and appreciation that once felt scarce.

By identifying the need beneath the emotion, you gain the ability to respond more directly.

For example, if fear appears before a challenging task, the need might involve encouragement or reassurance. Instead of ignoring the fear or forcing yourself forward harshly, you can provide the support that helps the nervous system remain steady.

Corrective rituals are another way to strengthen the reparenting process.

A corrective ritual is a small, intentional action that symbolically provides the emotional experience that may have been missing earlier in life. These rituals are not about pretending the past was different. They are about creating new experiences in the present that communicate safety and care to the emotional system.

For instance, someone who grew up without consistent encouragement might create a daily practice of acknowledging their efforts and progress. This could involve writing a short reflection each evening about something they handled well during the day.

Another person who experienced emotional neglect might establish a ritual of checking in with themselves each morning.

They might ask how they feel, what they need, and what would help them move through the day with greater balance.

These rituals gradually reshape emotional expectations. The inner child begins to experience attention and support where silence or dismissal once existed.

Inner dialogues deepen this process even further.

Inner dialogue involves consciously allowing different parts of your emotional world to speak to each other. One part may express fear, sadness, or anger, while another part responds with curiosity and guidance.

At first this may feel unusual, but it reflects a natural psychological process. The mind is composed of many internal voices representing different experiences and needs. Inner dialogue simply brings those voices into awareness.

Imagine noticing anxiety before a difficult conversation. Instead of suppressing the feeling, you might ask the anxious part of yourself what it fears. The response may reveal concerns about rejection or misunderstanding.

The adult part of you can then respond with reassurance: "I understand why this feels risky, but we can handle this situation carefully. I will stay present and respectful."

Through this exchange, the emotion receives acknowledgment while also being guided toward a balanced response.

Fear, shame, and emotional hunger often soften when they are met with this kind of attention.

Fear loses some of its urgency when the adult self offers stability. Shame begins to dissolve when compassion replaces judgment.

Emotional hunger decreases when the inner world begins providing consistent care.

These practices do not eliminate emotions completely. Instead, they transform the relationship you have with them.

Gradually, the inner environment becomes more nurturing. Instead of a place where mistakes lead to criticism and vulnerability leads to embarrassment, the mind becomes a space where emotions can appear without fear of rejection.

This shift creates a foundation for deeper healing.

Chapter 7 — Rewrite Core Beliefs

7.1 The Hidden Scripts That Guide Your Life

By the time someone reaches adulthood, many of their emotional reactions feel automatic. Certain situations immediately trigger doubt, fear, defensiveness, or the urge to prove oneself. A person may enter relationships expecting rejection, approach challenges with constant pressure to perform, or feel uneasy when someone offers genuine care.

These reactions often appear without clear explanation. People sometimes describe them as instincts or personality traits. They may say things like, "I've always been this way," or "That's just how I react."

Yet beneath these reactions usually lies something deeper: a set of core beliefs.

Core beliefs are the fundamental assumptions we hold about ourselves, other people, and the world around us. They develop gradually, often during childhood, when the mind is learning how relationships work and what conditions lead to safety or rejection.

Unlike passing thoughts, core beliefs operate quietly in the background. They influence how we interpret events, how we expect others to behave, and how we respond emotionally when something unexpected happens.

Because these beliefs form early and operate beneath conscious awareness, they can feel like simple truths rather than interpretations.

Someone who carries the belief "I am not enough" may not think of it as a belief at all. Instead, it may feel like an obvious fact. The mind begins interpreting everyday situations through that lens, reinforcing the assumption again and again.

Understanding core beliefs is essential because they function like emotional filters.

Every experience that passes through the mind is interpreted according to these filters. When a situation occurs, the brain does not analyze it in a neutral way. It quickly evaluates the event based on existing beliefs about worth, safety, and belonging.

If the core belief suggests that love must be earned through performance, then praise may feel temporary and mistakes may feel threatening. If the belief suggests that emotional expression leads to rejection, vulnerability may trigger anxiety even in supportive relationships.

The event itself may not be the true source of the reaction. The reaction often comes from the belief interpreting the event.

To see how this works, imagine someone who carries the belief "I am too much."

This belief often develops in environments where emotional expression was discouraged or where strong feelings were met with discomfort from caregivers. A child who cried frequently, asked many questions, or needed reassurance might have heard comments suggesting they were dramatic or demanding.

Over time, the child may conclude that their natural emotional needs are excessive.

As an adult, this belief can influence many aspects of life. The person may hesitate to express concerns in relationships because they fear being overwhelming. They might minimize their feelings during conversations or apologize for needing support.

Even when someone invites emotional honesty, the belief whispers a warning: if you share too much, you will push people away.

Another common core belief is "I am not enough."

This belief often forms when a child receives frequent criticism or when approval is closely tied to achievement. If praise appears only after exceptional performance, the child may learn that ordinary effort is not sufficient to earn appreciation.

The mind absorbs the message that worth depends on constant improvement.

In adulthood, this belief may appear as relentless self-pressure. Even when accomplishments are recognized, the satisfaction fades quickly because the belief continues asking for more proof. The person may struggle to relax or feel proud of their progress.

Every challenge becomes another test of worth.

A related belief suggests that love must be earned.

Children naturally assume that the behavior of caregivers reflects something about themselves. If affection is unpredictable or conditional, the child may attempt to adjust their behavior to restore connection.

They may become especially helpful, obedient, or high-achieving in hopes of maintaining approval.

Over time, the child may internalize the idea that love is not given freely. Instead, it must be secured through performance or constant attentiveness to others' needs.

In adulthood, this belief can shape relationship dynamics. Someone may feel responsible for maintaining harmony at all times. They may work hard to avoid conflict or prioritize others' comfort above their own.

When a relationship becomes stable and supportive, the belief may still create anxiety. The person may worry that if they stop proving their value, the connection will fade.

These beliefs do not develop because children misunderstand reality. They develop because children are trying to make sense of their emotional environment.

The developing mind constantly asks questions such as: What do I need to do to stay connected? What leads to approval? What leads to rejection?

The answers to those questions gradually become internal rules.

Sometimes the rules are accurate and helpful. In supportive environments, children may develop beliefs such as "My feelings matter" or "Mistakes are part of learning."

But when environments contain criticism, unpredictability, neglect, or emotional confusion, the rules may become restrictive.

The child adapts by creating beliefs that explain their experiences and help them navigate relationships as safely as possible.

Once formed, these beliefs influence expectations.

For example, someone who believes they are unworthy of consistent care may feel uneasy when others treat them with kindness. The experience contradicts the belief, so the mind searches for signs that the kindness will disappear.

Similarly, someone who believes conflict leads to rejection may avoid expressing disagreement even in relationships where open communication would actually strengthen trust.

Core beliefs do not only influence behavior. They shape emotional anticipation.

Before a conversation even begins, the belief may predict how the situation will unfold. Before attempting a new challenge, the belief may quietly suggest that failure is likely.

These predictions influence choices.

A person who believes they are not capable may hesitate to pursue opportunities that could challenge that assumption. Someone who believes they are difficult to love may tolerate unhealthy relationships because they assume better treatment is unlikely.

Over time, these choices reinforce the original belief.

If someone avoids opportunities, they may never experience the success that would challenge the idea of inadequacy. If someone remains in relationships where their needs are ignored, they may continue gathering evidence that their needs do not matter.

This process creates a self-perpetuating cycle.

Breaking that cycle begins with awareness.

The first step in rewriting core beliefs is learning to detect them. Because these beliefs often operate silently, they can be difficult to recognize at first.

One helpful approach is paying attention to moments of strong emotional reaction.

When an event triggers intense shame, anxiety, or defensiveness, it often touches a core belief. For example, a small criticism may trigger a wave of self-doubt that feels disproportionate to the situation. Beneath the reaction may be the belief that mistakes reveal personal inadequacy.

Similarly, when someone struggles to accept kindness or support, it may signal a belief that care must be earned or that vulnerability is unsafe.

Another way to detect core beliefs is by noticing recurring thoughts.

Statements that begin with phrases like "I always," "I never," or "people will eventually" often reveal underlying assumptions. These thoughts may appear during moments of stress or reflection, revealing the stories the mind tells about identity and relationships.

Once these beliefs become visible, they can be examined rather than accepted automatically.

This process does not involve immediately replacing old beliefs with positive affirmations. Real change requires understanding where the belief came from and how it has shaped behavior over time.

The purpose of this chapter is to bring these hidden scripts into awareness.

When you begin recognizing the beliefs that influence your reactions, choices, and expectations, you gain the ability to question them. What once felt like unquestionable truth begins to appear as a story that formed under specific circumstances.

And once a belief is seen clearly, the process of rewriting it can begin.

7.2 Challenging the Beliefs That No Longer Serve You

Once core beliefs become visible, a new question naturally follows: if these beliefs were formed long ago, can they actually change?

The answer is yes, but the process is more nuanced than many people expect.

Core beliefs cannot simply be erased by deciding to think differently. They are deeply embedded emotional interpretations formed over years of repeated experiences. The mind does not release them easily because, from its perspective, these beliefs once helped protect you from pain or confusion.

Trying to replace them instantly with positive statements often creates resistance.

For example, someone who carries the belief "I am not enough" may try repeating phrases such as "I am perfect the way I am." While the statement may sound encouraging, the emotional system may reject it because it contradicts years of internal evidence. The mind senses a gap between the affirmation and lived experience.

This is why effective belief change involves something deeper than repetition of optimistic language. It requires emotional re-education.

Emotional re-education means teaching the mind new interpretations through evidence, reflection, and experience. Instead of forcing the mind to accept unrealistic statements, the goal is to gradually introduce perspectives that are more accurate and balanced.

The first step in this process is questioning the belief.

When a core belief becomes conscious, you can begin examining its origin and accuracy. This does not mean arguing aggressively with yourself. Instead, it involves gentle curiosity about whether the belief truly represents reality.

Consider someone who believes they are too much for others. When that belief appears, they might ask themselves when they first began feeling that way. Often the answer leads back to specific situations where emotional expression was discouraged or misunderstood.

Recognizing the origin of the belief helps reveal that it was shaped by particular circumstances rather than universal truth.

The next step involves examining evidence.

The mind tends to collect evidence that supports existing beliefs while ignoring evidence that contradicts them. Someone who believes they are inadequate may focus heavily on mistakes while overlooking moments of competence or appreciation.

Challenging a belief involves intentionally expanding the range of evidence considered.

This does not mean searching only for positive examples. Instead, it means looking at experiences with greater honesty and balance. A person might ask themselves whether there have been moments when others valued their presence, appreciated their work, or responded warmly to their vulnerability.

These experiences may have been overlooked or dismissed in the past because they did not fit the belief.

By acknowledging them, the mind begins encountering information that challenges the original assumption.

Another useful practice involves identifying distortions within the belief.

Many core beliefs rely on exaggerated conclusions. Words such as "always," "never," or "everyone" often appear in these internal narratives. For instance, someone might think, "I always disappoint people," or "No one really cares about what I feel."

These statements feel convincing because they capture emotional intensity, but they rarely reflect objective reality.

Examining the language of the belief can reveal these distortions. When you slow down and consider whether the belief applies in every situation or with every person, the rigid structure begins to soften.

The belief may transform from "I always disappoint people" into something more accurate, such as "There have been moments when I disappointed someone, and that felt painful."

This shift might seem subtle, but it changes the emotional meaning significantly. The original belief defines identity, while the revised statement describes a specific experience.

Over time, these adjustments create space for new interpretations.

Replacing a distorted belief requires identifying a grounded alternative. The new belief must feel realistic enough that the emotional system can gradually accept it.

For example, someone who once believed "Love must be earned" might develop a new understanding such as "Healthy relationships include care that is not dependent on perfection." This statement acknowledges the complexity of relationships without denying the need for effort and respect.

The new belief becomes a hypothesis rather than a forced conclusion.

At this stage, the mind begins testing the new perspective against real experiences.

Perhaps a friend offers support during a difficult moment without expecting anything in return. Perhaps a partner responds with understanding when a mistake occurs. Each of these experiences provides evidence that challenges the earlier belief.

Over time, the mind learns that the old assumption does not fully describe reality.

This process resembles learning a new language. At first the unfamiliar words feel awkward and uncertain. With repeated exposure and practice, they become easier to use.

Belief change follows a similar pattern.

The emotional system requires repeated encounters with new evidence before it begins trusting a different interpretation. Each time the new belief is supported by experience, its influence grows slightly stronger.

Gradually, the old belief loses its dominance.

The goal of this process is not perfection. Even as new beliefs develop, old patterns may occasionally resurface. What matters is that the mind now recognizes those patterns as interpretations rather than unquestionable truths.

This awareness opens the door to change.

Chapter 8 — Heal Relationship Patterns

8.1 How Inner Wounds Shape Outer Connections

Relationships are the places where emotional patterns become most visible. A person may spend years believing they have resolved certain personal struggles, only to notice those same reactions appearing again when they grow close to someone else. In friendships, romantic partnerships, family dynamics, and professional environments, the emotional system is constantly interacting with other people's behaviors, expectations, and moods. These interactions activate the beliefs, coping strategies, and protective responses that were formed earlier in life.

Because relationships involve vulnerability and connection, they often trigger the deepest emotional patterns. Situations that resemble earlier experiences—whether consciously recognized or not—can awaken the same fears or defenses that once helped protect a younger self. Someone who learned that conflict leads to rejection may avoid disagreement even when it would lead to healthy understanding. Another person who once felt invisible may work tirelessly to prove their value in relationships, giving more than they receive in hopes of maintaining connection.

These patterns rarely appear deliberately. Most individuals enter relationships hoping for closeness, mutual support, and emotional safety. Yet unhealed wounds quietly influence the way people interpret interactions and respond to others. The result is that many relationship challenges are not caused only by the present moment, but also by emotional history.

Conflict is one of the clearest examples of this process.

Disagreements are natural in any relationship. People have different needs, expectations, and ways of expressing themselves. When emotional wounds remain unaddressed, however, conflict can feel far more threatening than it actually is. A conversation that begins as a simple difference of opinion may quickly activate deeper fears.

Someone who carries a wound related to criticism may interpret feedback as a personal attack. Even constructive suggestions might trigger defensiveness or shame. The person may respond by arguing intensely, withdrawing emotionally, or attempting to justify themselves in great detail.

Another individual may react to conflict by shutting down entirely. If earlier experiences taught them that arguments lead to emotional distance or instability, their nervous system may attempt to avoid the situation altogether. Instead of expressing their perspective, they retreat inward, hoping the tension will disappear without direct discussion.

These reactions can confuse both people involved. The conversation that one person sees as a normal exchange of ideas may feel like a threat to the other. Without understanding the emotional patterns beneath these responses, both individuals may begin blaming each other for the conflict.

Overgiving is another common relationship pattern connected to unhealed wounds.

Many people develop the habit of prioritizing others' needs while neglecting their own. This pattern often grows from earlier environments where approval or affection seemed conditional. The child may have learned that being helpful, agreeable, or accommodating increased the chances of maintaining connection.

As adults, individuals with this pattern may invest enormous energy into supporting others. They listen carefully, anticipate needs, and offer help without hesitation. On the surface, this behavior can appear generous and caring.

However, when overgiving becomes the primary way someone seeks connection, it often leads to imbalance. The person may feel exhausted, resentful, or unappreciated because their efforts are rarely matched. They may also struggle to ask for support themselves, fearing that doing so would appear selfish or demanding.

The deeper issue is not generosity itself but the belief that worth depends on constant giving.

Healing this pattern requires recognizing that healthy relationships include reciprocity. Support flows in both directions rather than resting entirely on one person's shoulders.

Emotional withdrawal represents another way wounds influence relationships.

When closeness feels risky, the mind may create distance as a form of protection. Someone who experienced rejection or emotional instability earlier in life may find intimacy uncomfortable. Even when they care deeply about others, they may hold back parts of themselves.

This withdrawal can appear in subtle ways. A person might avoid discussing personal feelings, change the subject when conversations become vulnerable, or maintain emotional independence to an extreme degree. They may believe they are protecting themselves from potential disappointment.

The challenge is that emotional distance also prevents genuine connection.

Partners or friends may interpret the withdrawal as lack of interest or trust. They may attempt to draw closer, which can make the withdrawing person feel even more pressured. Without awareness of the underlying wound, both individuals can become trapped in a cycle of misunderstanding.

Fear of vulnerability often accompanies these patterns.

Opening up emotionally requires trust. It means allowing another person to see fears, insecurities, and desires that might not always feel comfortable to share. For someone whose earlier experiences involved rejection or dismissal, vulnerability can feel dangerous.

The mind may anticipate that revealing emotions will lead to judgment, abandonment, or disappointment. As a result, the person may carefully manage what they share, presenting only the parts of themselves that feel safe or acceptable.

While this strategy protects against immediate discomfort, it also prevents the deeper intimacy that relationships thrive on.

Healing relationship patterns begins with recognizing how these emotional responses developed.

When you understand that conflict avoidance, overgiving, withdrawal, or fear of vulnerability were once protective strategies, self-blame begins to soften. The patterns were attempts to maintain safety in environments where certain needs were uncertain or misunderstood.

However, those strategies may no longer serve the life you are building today.

Inner work gradually transforms how these patterns appear in relationships. As core beliefs shift and emotional regulation strengthens, the individual becomes more capable of responding to situations from the perspective of their present self rather than from the protective reactions of the past.

For example, someone who once avoided conflict may begin expressing concerns calmly and directly. Instead of interpreting disagreement as a threat to the relationship, they learn to view it as an opportunity for clarity and mutual understanding.

A person who previously overgave may start noticing their own needs more clearly. They might practice asking for support, expressing preferences, or setting limits around how much energy they offer to others.

These changes do not happen overnight. Relationship patterns often developed over many years, and shifting them requires patience. But each moment of awareness creates an opportunity for a different response.

Communication becomes a key part of this transformation.

When individuals begin recognizing their emotional patterns, they can share that awareness with others in thoughtful ways. Instead of reacting impulsively, they might explain what they are experiencing internally.

For instance, someone might say that conflict sometimes makes them anxious because of earlier experiences, but they are working on staying present in the conversation. This type of openness can help partners or friends understand reactions that might otherwise seem confusing.

Healthy relationships often become powerful spaces for healing.

When people respond with patience, empathy, and respect, they provide experiences that challenge old beliefs about connection.

A person who once feared rejection may discover that honesty strengthens relationships rather than weakening them.

At the same time, inner work helps individuals recognize when a relationship environment is not supportive of growth. If certain connections repeatedly involve disrespect, manipulation, or emotional instability, the individual may need to reconsider how much influence those relationships have in their life.

Healing relationship patterns does not mean staying in every relationship or fixing every conflict. It means developing the awareness and emotional skill needed to participate in connections more consciously.

As inner understanding deepens, the outer dynamics of relationships begin to shift.

The person who once felt powerless in emotional interactions gradually discovers greater choice. They can respond rather than react, communicate rather than withdraw, and connect rather than overcompensate.

Through this process, relationships become less about repeating old wounds and more about building new experiences of trust, balance, and mutual respect.

8.2 Learning to Communicate With Emotional Intelligence

Once a person begins understanding their emotional patterns, a new challenge appears: how to express that awareness in relationships. Insight alone does not change relationship dynamics unless it influences communication. The way people speak, listen, and respond during emotional moments determines whether old patterns continue repeating or whether healthier interactions begin to develop.

Communication rooted in emotional intelligence requires more than simply speaking honestly. It involves recognizing emotions as they arise, expressing needs clearly, and listening to others without immediately defending oneself. These skills allow conversations to remain constructive even when the topic is sensitive.

One of the most important elements of emotionally intelligent communication is naming feelings.

Many conflicts escalate because emotions remain unspoken or are expressed indirectly. Instead of acknowledging feelings openly, people often communicate through accusations or assumptions. For example, someone who feels hurt might say, "You never care about what I think." The statement may express genuine pain, but it frames the conversation as a judgment about the other person's character.

When communication begins with accusation, the listener's natural response is defensiveness. Instead of hearing the underlying emotion, they focus on defending themselves against the criticism.

Naming feelings changes the tone of the conversation.

When someone says, "I felt hurt when that happened," the focus shifts from blame to experience. The statement does not claim to know the other person's intentions. It simply shares what occurred internally.

This distinction is subtle but powerful. It allows the listener to understand the emotional impact of a situation without feeling immediately attacked.

Developing the habit of naming feelings requires practice. Many people were not encouraged to identify or express emotions clearly during childhood. As a result, they may struggle to distinguish between similar feelings such as disappointment, frustration, embarrassment, or sadness.

The more familiar a person becomes with their emotional vocabulary, the easier it becomes to communicate honestly without exaggeration or accusation.

Expressing needs is another essential skill.

Feelings often arise because a particular need has not been met. When those needs remain hidden, the conversation may revolve around surface-level complaints instead of addressing the real issue.

Imagine a situation where someone feels upset because a friend canceled plans. Without awareness of the underlying need, they might express irritation or withdraw from contact. The friend may assume the reaction is excessive without understanding the emotional context.

If the individual recognizes that the deeper need involves reliability or reassurance, the conversation can become more constructive. They might say that they value time together and felt disappointed because the change was unexpected.

This type of communication invites understanding rather than conflict.

Expressing needs does not guarantee that every request will be fulfilled. However, it allows both individuals to understand what matters to each other. When needs remain unspoken, misunderstandings often multiply.

Listening without defensiveness is equally important.

During emotional conversations, people frequently focus on preparing their response rather than truly hearing what the other person is saying. If the conversation involves criticism or disagreement, the mind may quickly shift into protective mode.

Defensiveness is a natural reaction when someone feels judged or misunderstood. Yet it often prevents meaningful dialogue. Instead of exploring the concern being raised, the conversation becomes a debate about who is right.

Emotionally intelligent listening requires a temporary suspension of self-defense.

This does not mean accepting blame for things that are untrue. It simply means creating space to understand the other person's experience before responding.

When someone expresses a concern, a helpful response may involve reflecting what was heard rather than immediately explaining or correcting. For example, you might acknowledge that the situation made them feel ignored or frustrated.

This acknowledgment does not necessarily mean you agree with their interpretation. It demonstrates that their feelings have been heard.

When people feel understood, their emotional intensity often decreases. This makes it easier for both individuals to discuss solutions rather than defending positions.

Replacing reactive patterns with mature relational habits takes time.

Many reactions in relationships occur automatically because they were practiced repeatedly in earlier environments. Someone who learned to respond to conflict with silence may instinctively withdraw. Another person who experienced frequent criticism may react quickly with defensiveness.

Emotional intelligence introduces a pause between feeling and response.

When tension appears, the individual becomes aware of their internal reaction before acting on it. This awareness allows them to choose how to communicate rather than repeating the same pattern.

Over time, this pause becomes a new habit.

Instead of escalating conflict, the person can express emotions calmly, ask clarifying questions, and remain present during difficult conversations. The goal is not to eliminate disagreement but to transform how disagreement is handled.

Healthy communication reduces repeated conflicts because it addresses the underlying emotions and needs involved in a situation. When both individuals feel heard and respected, the relationship becomes a space for collaboration rather than competition.

Chapter 9 — Face Setbacks Wisely

9.1 When Progress Feels Like Going Backward

At some point in any healing process, a moment arrives that can feel discouraging. After weeks or months of reflection, emotional awareness, and intentional change, an old reaction suddenly appears again. A familiar fear resurfaces during a relationship conflict. A harsh inner voice returns after a mistake. A situation that once seemed manageable suddenly triggers the same anxiety or withdrawal that existed before the work began.

For many people, these moments create immediate doubt. They begin wondering whether any progress has actually occurred. The mind may quickly produce thoughts such as, "I thought I had moved past this," or "Why am I back in the same place again?"

These reactions are understandable, but they often misunderstand how emotional healing actually works.

Healing rarely follows a straight path.

Many people expect growth to look like a steady upward line, where each step moves further away from past patterns and closer to permanent stability. In reality, emotional growth tends to unfold more like a series of expanding circles. As awareness increases, deeper layers of experience gradually come into view.

What feels like regression is often the discovery of something that was not visible before.

Early in the healing process, the mind may focus on the most obvious patterns. Someone might begin noticing how they react to criticism or how they avoid conflict. As they practice emotional awareness and compassion, those patterns may soften.

But over time, new situations arise that reveal more subtle layers of the same wound.

For example, a person who once reacted strongly to criticism might learn to handle feedback calmly in professional settings. Later, they might notice that the same sensitivity appears in intimate relationships where emotional vulnerability feels greater.

This does not mean the earlier progress was false. It simply means the work is reaching deeper into areas that carry stronger emotional significance.

The mind and nervous system reveal experiences gradually, often in the order that feels safest to process.

This pattern is similar to how physical healing unfolds. When someone recovers from an injury, they may feel strong during certain movements but still experience discomfort in others. Each new activity reveals areas that require additional attention.

Emotional healing follows a similar rhythm.

Moments that appear to be setbacks often signal that the system is ready to address a new layer of understanding.

Regression can also occur when the nervous system encounters stress or unfamiliar circumstances.

Even after significant progress, situations that resemble earlier experiences may activate protective responses automatically. The brain is designed to prioritize safety, and it tends to rely on familiar reactions during moments of uncertainty.

For instance, someone who has worked extensively on expressing emotions may still feel the urge to withdraw during an especially intense conversation. The body remembers how withdrawal once helped create distance from discomfort.

In these moments, the goal is not to eliminate the reaction entirely. The goal is to recognize it sooner and respond with greater awareness.

The difference between past behavior and present growth often lies in the pause.

Previously, the reaction might have occurred automatically and remained unexamined. Now, the person notices it happening. They may reflect afterward, asking what triggered the response and what emotional need might have been present.

This awareness represents meaningful progress.

Another important reason setbacks occur is that healing often disrupts familiar identities.

Many people build their sense of self around coping strategies that helped them navigate difficult environments. Someone who learned to stay strong and independent may take pride in never needing help. Another person who learned to please others may feel valued for being dependable and accommodating.

As healing progresses, these identities begin to shift.

The person may start setting boundaries, expressing vulnerability, or prioritizing their own needs. While these changes support long-term well-being, they can also create temporary discomfort.

Part of the mind may resist the change because the old identity once provided a sense of certainty.

During these periods of adjustment, emotional confusion may appear. The individual may feel unsure about how to respond in situations where the old pattern no longer feels appropriate but the new response has not yet become fully comfortable.

This uncertainty is not a sign of failure. It is evidence that the healing process is actively reshaping internal patterns.

Moments of discouragement can also arise when people compare their progress to unrealistic expectations.

Popular narratives about personal growth sometimes suggest that once someone gains insight into their past, their emotional patterns will change quickly and permanently. When reality does not match that expectation, individuals may assume they are doing something wrong.

In truth, meaningful change often unfolds slowly.

The mind and nervous system require repeated experiences before new patterns become stable. Just as muscles strengthen through consistent practice, emotional responses change through repeated awareness and compassionate action.

Each time you recognize an old reaction and choose a different response—even if that response occurs later than you hoped— you are reinforcing a new pathway.

Gradually, these pathways become more natural.

Another helpful perspective involves viewing setbacks as information rather than obstacles.

When an old pattern appears, it offers valuable insight into the situations or emotions that still require attention. Instead of treating the experience as a mistake, it can become a source of learning.

You might ask questions such as: What triggered this reaction? What belief or fear might have been activated? What support or boundary might have helped in that moment?

These reflections transform setbacks into opportunities for deeper understanding.

Self-compassion becomes especially important during these times.

When people respond to setbacks with harsh criticism, the emotional system often becomes more defensive. Shame and frustration can make it harder to reflect calmly on what happened.

In contrast, approaching the moment with compassion creates space for growth.

Instead of saying, "I failed again," the internal dialogue might shift toward curiosity: "Something important happened here. What can I learn from this experience?"

This shift does not excuse harmful behavior, but it prevents the mind from becoming trapped in self-blame.

It also reminds the inner child that mistakes do not lead to rejection.

Many emotional wounds developed in environments where errors or vulnerability were met with criticism or withdrawal. Responding to setbacks with kindness provides a different experience—one where learning is encouraged rather than punished.

Over time, this compassionate response strengthens resilience.

The individual begins trusting that difficult moments can be navigated without losing progress. They understand that emotional growth involves cycles of reflection, adjustment, and renewed effort.

Gradually, the fear of setbacks decreases.

Instead of interpreting them as signs that healing has stopped, the person learns to see them as part of the process. Each challenge becomes an opportunity to practice the skills developed throughout the journey.

In this way, setbacks transform from obstacles into teachers.

They reveal where compassion is still needed, where boundaries may require reinforcement, and where deeper understanding can emerge.

Healing becomes less about achieving a perfect emotional state and more about developing the ability to respond to life's complexities with patience, awareness, and courage.

9.2 When Understanding Isn't the Same as Change

As people move deeper into emotional work, they often encounter internal objections that slow or interrupt the process. These objections are not signs that someone is incapable of healing. In many cases, they are protective responses from the mind attempting to maintain familiar patterns.

Emotional change involves stepping into uncertainty. Old beliefs and coping strategies may have caused difficulty, but they were also predictable. When those patterns begin to shift, the mind sometimes reacts with hesitation or skepticism. Certain thoughts appear that seem logical on the surface but actually function as barriers to progress.

One common thought is: "I already understand this."

Insight can feel powerful. When someone recognizes how a childhood experience shaped their reactions or identifies the belief behind a pattern, it may seem as though the problem has been solved. Understanding provides clarity, and clarity often brings relief.

However, insight alone does not automatically transform emotional habits.

The brain can understand something intellectually while still reacting emotionally in the same way it did before. A person may fully recognize that their fear of rejection comes from earlier experiences, yet still feel the same anxiety when someone becomes distant.

This gap between understanding and change can be frustrating.

The key is recognizing that emotional learning happens through repetition and experience rather than insight alone. Intellectual awareness opens the door, but the nervous system needs time and practice to build new responses.

When someone believes they already understand everything necessary, they may unintentionally stop engaging with the practices that create change. The process becomes a mental exercise instead of an emotional one.

Another common thought appears in a different form: "My past was not that bad."

Many people hesitate to explore their emotional history because they compare their experiences with more extreme stories they have heard. They may believe that unless they experienced dramatic trauma, their struggles are not significant enough to examine.

This perspective often leads to minimization.

Minimization occurs when individuals dismiss the emotional impact of their experiences because they believe others had it worse. While empathy for others is valuable, comparing pain rarely leads to healing.

Emotional wounds do not depend only on the severity of events. They also depend on how a child interpreted those experiences and whether their emotional needs were supported at the time.

Two children can live in similar environments and develop very different emotional responses depending on personality, temperament, and the presence of supportive relationships.

When someone repeatedly tells themselves that their experiences were not significant enough to matter, they may silence important emotional signals. The mind learns to ignore discomfort rather than investigate it.

Healing requires acknowledging that emotional experiences deserve attention regardless of how they compare to others.

Another barrier appears in the thought: "I don't know where to start."

The work of examining emotional patterns can feel overwhelming, especially when someone is aware that many aspects of their life have been influenced by earlier experiences. The idea of addressing everything at once may create paralysis.

This reaction often comes from the belief that healing requires a perfect starting point.

In reality, progress usually begins with the smallest moments of awareness. It may start with noticing how you speak to yourself after making a mistake. It may involve recognizing tension during a conversation or identifying the belief behind a recurring fear.

Each moment of observation provides information that can guide the next step.

When the mind insists on knowing the entire path before beginning, it may be trying to avoid uncertainty. Yet emotional growth unfolds through exploration rather than precise planning.

Fear is often present beneath these objections.

Insight may feel safer than action because it allows distance from difficult emotions. Minimizing the past may protect against feelings that have not yet been fully acknowledged. Hesitation about where to start may reflect concern about confronting unfamiliar parts of the self.

These responses are understandable.

The mind developed protective strategies long ago to manage emotional discomfort. When healing begins, those strategies sometimes attempt to maintain their role.

Recognizing these barriers allows you to approach them with curiosity rather than frustration.

If you notice the thought that you already understand everything, you might ask whether the insight has been applied consistently in daily life. If you notice yourself minimizing past experiences, you might explore what emotions arise when you allow those memories to matter.

If you feel uncertain about where to begin, you might simply start with the next moment of awareness rather than waiting for a complete roadmap.

Progress often begins when people stop trying to eliminate uncertainty and instead learn how to move forward with it.

Chapter 10 — Live Emotionally Free

10.1 Bringing Healing Into Everyday Life

After exploring emotional patterns, childhood wounds, beliefs, and relationship dynamics, a natural question begins to emerge: what does life actually look like once this work begins to integrate? Many people assume emotional healing leads to a permanent state of calm or confidence, as if difficult emotions disappear entirely once the right insights are discovered.

In reality, emotional freedom does not mean the absence of fear, sadness, or uncertainty. These feelings are part of being human. What changes is the way they are understood and the way a person responds when they appear.

Integration is the stage where emotional intelligence and inner child healing move beyond reflection and become part of daily living. Instead of existing only as ideas or exercises, the principles learned throughout the journey begin shaping decisions, habits, boundaries, and identity.

At first, the changes may appear subtle.

Someone who once reacted quickly during conflict may notice a brief pause before speaking. A person who previously criticized themselves harshly after mistakes may respond with curiosity instead of shame. Another individual who once ignored emotional needs may begin asking themselves what support or rest would help them feel balanced.

These moments may seem small, but they represent a profound shift.

In earlier stages of life, emotional reactions were often driven by automatic patterns formed during childhood. When those patterns are examined and gradually reshaped, the individual begins responding from awareness rather than from survival strategies.

This awareness influences everyday decisions.

Imagine someone who previously believed their worth depended on constant productivity. For years, they may have pushed themselves relentlessly, rarely allowing time for rest or reflection. Through emotional work, they begin recognizing how that belief developed and how it affects their well-being.

Integration does not simply involve recognizing the belief. It involves making choices that reflect a new understanding.

They may begin protecting time for recovery, trusting that rest supports long-term growth rather than threatening their value. They may approach challenges with determination but without the relentless pressure that once dominated their thinking.

Over time, these decisions reshape habits.

Habits are the daily expressions of beliefs and priorities. When emotional awareness increases, habits begin aligning with the values that support well-being.

For example, someone who once avoided difficult conversations may develop the habit of addressing concerns calmly and directly. Another person who previously prioritized others' needs at the expense of their own may begin checking in with themselves before agreeing to new commitments.

These habits may feel unfamiliar at first. Change often involves stepping outside the comfort of established routines.

However, repetition gradually transforms these choices into natural responses. What once required conscious effort becomes a normal part of how the person moves through the world.

Boundaries also evolve during this stage.

Earlier chapters explored how emotional wounds often lead people to tolerate situations that undermine their well-being. A fear of rejection might prevent someone from expressing their needs, while a desire for approval might encourage overgiving in relationships.

As healing progresses, boundaries become clearer.

The individual learns to recognize when a situation creates unnecessary emotional strain and begins responding accordingly. This may involve declining invitations that lead to exhaustion, communicating limits within relationships, or choosing environments that support emotional stability.

Setting boundaries is not about rejecting connection. It is about protecting the conditions that allow genuine connection to exist.

When boundaries are respected, relationships become healthier and more balanced. The individual no longer feels responsible for managing everyone else's emotions while ignoring their own.

Identity begins shifting as well.

For many people, emotional wounds shaped how they viewed themselves for years. They may have seen themselves as overly sensitive, difficult, or inadequate. These conclusions were often formed during moments when their emotional needs were misunderstood or dismissed.

As the healing process unfolds, those interpretations gradually lose their influence.

The individual begins seeing themselves with greater accuracy. Instead of defining themselves by old coping strategies, they recognize the resilience and intelligence that allowed them to navigate difficult circumstances.

This new perspective supports a more stable sense of identity.

Rather than relying on external validation to determine worth, the person develops an internal understanding of their value. They no longer need to prove themselves constantly because their sense of self is grounded in awareness rather than approval.

Relationships reflect this shift.

When someone approaches connections from a place of emotional stability, the dynamics naturally change. Instead of repeating patterns of overgiving, withdrawal, or fear of vulnerability, the individual begins participating in relationships with greater honesty and balance.

They communicate needs openly and listen to others with empathy. They allow themselves to be seen without feeling compelled to hide parts of their experience.

This openness encourages deeper connection.

At the same time, emotional awareness increases discernment. The person becomes more attentive to the qualities that define healthy relationships—mutual respect, willingness to communicate, and shared responsibility for emotional well-being.

Connections that support growth are nurtured, while those that consistently undermine it may gradually lose their central role.

Another important aspect of integration involves how individuals respond to their own emotions.

Earlier in life, emotions may have felt overwhelming or confusing. A strong reaction could trigger self-criticism or avoidance. Healing transforms this relationship.

When emotions arise, the individual becomes curious about their meaning. They recognize feelings as signals rather than threats.

If sadness appears, it may point toward a need for comfort or reflection. If anger surfaces, it may indicate that a boundary has been crossed. If anxiety arises, it may highlight uncertainty that deserves attention.

Instead of resisting these signals, the person learns to respond with awareness.

Over time, this approach creates a sense of emotional freedom.

Freedom does not mean controlling every feeling or ensuring that life remains comfortable. It means having the ability to navigate emotional experiences without losing connection to oneself.

Challenges still occur. Difficult conversations still happen. Uncertainty and disappointment remain part of the human experience.

But the individual no longer feels trapped by those moments.

They have developed tools to reflect, regulate, and respond with intention.

Integration also includes accepting that growth continues throughout life.

Healing is not a destination where every emotional pattern disappears permanently. It is an ongoing process of awareness and adjustment.

New experiences may reveal layers of understanding that were not visible before. Relationships may evolve in ways that challenge existing beliefs. Personal goals may shift as identity continues developing.

The difference is that the individual now possesses a foundation for navigating these changes.

Instead of feeling lost during emotional challenges, they return to the principles that supported their growth: awareness, compassion, reflection, and honest communication.

These principles act as guides rather than rules.

They help the individual remain connected to themselves even when circumstances change.

Living emotionally free means carrying these practices into everyday life. It means recognizing that healing is not confined to moments of reflection or therapy. It appears in daily choices, conversations, and responses to uncertainty.

Each time someone chooses awareness instead of automatic reaction, compassion instead of criticism, or honesty instead of silence, the work of healing becomes part of the life they are building.

Over time, these choices create a new normal.

The emotional patterns that once defined survival gradually give way to patterns that support growth, connection, and authenticity.

This is what sustainable transformation looks like in practice.

10.2 Keeping Growth Alive Through Daily Practice

Integration becomes real when emotional awareness begins shaping daily life. Without consistent attention, even meaningful insights can slowly fade into the background. People often experience moments of clarity during reflection or reading, yet find themselves slipping back into familiar routines when life becomes busy again. This is not a failure of intention. It simply reflects how the mind works. Habits and emotional patterns are reinforced through repetition, and change remains stable when new habits are practiced consistently.

For this reason, emotional freedom is supported by routines that keep awareness active. These routines do not need to be complicated or time-consuming. In fact, the most sustainable practices are often the simplest ones repeated regularly. What matters is that they create moments where you pause long enough to reconnect with your emotional world.

Daily emotional check-ins are one of the most effective ways to maintain that connection. A check-in is simply a brief moment where you ask yourself what you are experiencing internally. Many people move through their days responding to tasks, conversations, and responsibilities without noticing what is happening emotionally. By the time they become aware of tension or sadness, the feeling may already be overwhelming.

A daily check-in interrupts this pattern. It might occur in the morning before the day begins, during a quiet moment in the afternoon, or at night before sleep. During that time you ask simple questions: What am I feeling right now? What has influenced my mood today? What might I need in this moment?

These questions encourage emotional awareness without pressure to find perfect answers. Sometimes the response will be clear. At other times the feeling may be vague or mixed. The purpose is not to analyze every emotion but to remain connected to the internal signals that guide well-being.

Repair rituals provide another valuable practice.

No matter how much growth someone experiences, misunderstandings and mistakes will still occur in relationships. A conversation may become tense, a boundary may be overlooked, or a reaction may appear before awareness has time to intervene. Repair rituals ensure that these moments do not become sources of lingering resentment or disconnection.

Repair involves acknowledging what happened and taking responsibility where appropriate. It may include apologizing for words spoken in frustration or clarifying intentions after a misunderstanding. Repair does not mean accepting blame for situations that are not yours to carry. It simply means recognizing that relationships remain healthy when people are willing to address mistakes openly.

When repair becomes a habit, relationships feel safer. People know that difficulties will not be ignored or allowed to grow into silent distance. Instead, they become opportunities to strengthen trust.

Reflection also plays an important role in maintaining emotional growth.

Reflection does not require long periods of analysis. Often a few minutes of quiet thought or writing can reveal patterns that would otherwise remain unnoticed. At the end of a day or week, you might consider moments that felt emotionally significant.

What situations brought satisfaction or peace? Which ones created tension or discomfort? How did you respond in those moments, and what might you try differently next time?

These reflections help transform everyday experiences into learning opportunities. Over time, patterns become clearer. You may notice that certain environments increase stress, while others support calm and creativity. You may recognize the situations where boundaries need strengthening or where vulnerability leads to deeper connection.

Reflection also allows you to recognize progress that might otherwise go unnoticed. Emotional growth often appears in subtle ways—a calmer response during conflict, a willingness to ask for help, or a decision to step away from an unhealthy situation. Without reflection, these changes can be easy to overlook.

Relational honesty keeps growth grounded in real life.

Many people can practice emotional awareness privately yet struggle to express their needs and experiences openly with others. Relational honesty involves bringing the same awareness developed internally into conversations and interactions.

This does not mean sharing every thought or feeling without consideration. Instead, it involves communicating important emotions and needs respectfully rather than hiding them out of fear or habit.

For example, if something in a relationship feels uncomfortable, relational honesty encourages addressing the issue calmly rather than suppressing it. If appreciation is felt, expressing it strengthens connection. If boundaries are necessary, communicating them clearly prevents confusion and resentment.

Over time, these practices create a rhythm of emotional health.

Daily check-ins maintain awareness. Repair rituals protect relationships from accumulating tension. Reflection supports learning and growth. Relational honesty strengthens connection and authenticity.

Together, these routines transform healing from an occasional activity into a lifestyle.

A healing lifestyle does not require perfection. There will be days when awareness feels effortless and others when emotions feel more challenging. What matters is the ongoing willingness to return to these practices.

Just as physical health benefits from regular movement and nourishment, emotional health grows through consistent attention and care.

When these routines become part of daily life, emotional intelligence remains active rather than theoretical. The lessons learned during healing continue shaping choices and interactions long after the initial work began.

Conclusion — Keep Becoming Whole

The journey you have just traveled through these pages began with a simple but profound question: why do we sometimes feel trapped in emotional patterns we do not fully understand? Many people arrive at this question after years of confusion, frustration, or quiet self-doubt. Reactions seem to repeat themselves. Relationships follow familiar cycles. Certain moments of criticism, rejection, or distance trigger emotions that feel far larger than the situation itself.

At the beginning of this journey, these experiences may have felt mysterious or even discouraging. Emotional responses might have seemed like flaws in personality or weaknesses that needed to be hidden or controlled. The mind may have tried to explain them away, suppress them, or judge them harshly.

Yet as you moved through the chapters of this book, a different picture began to emerge.

You explored how emotional patterns often develop as intelligent adaptations to earlier environments. The mind and nervous system learned strategies designed to maintain safety, connection, and belonging during childhood. These strategies were not random mistakes. They were responses created by a younger version of you who was trying to make sense of the world with the resources available at the time.

Understanding this truth changes the way emotional struggles are interpreted.

Instead of seeing yourself as someone who is broken or overly sensitive, you begin recognizing that your emotional responses carry history and meaning. Behind many reactions lies a younger part of you that once needed protection, reassurance, or understanding.

The concept of the inner child brought language to this experience. It revealed how memories of unmet needs, criticism, abandonment, or inconsistency can continue influencing the present. The patterns that once helped a child survive may still guide adult reactions long after the original circumstances have changed.

But this journey was never about remaining trapped in the past.

Through emotional intelligence, awareness, and compassion, you began discovering that these patterns can be understood and transformed. The process of healing involves recognizing what shaped you without allowing it to define who you will become.

This realization leads to one of the central messages of this work: healing is not about becoming someone else. It is about recovering parts of yourself that may have been hidden by fear, shame, or misunderstanding.

Many people approach emotional growth believing they must replace their identity with something entirely new. They imagine that healing means eliminating every difficult feeling or becoming permanently confident and calm.

In reality, wholeness emerges in a different way.

Wholeness appears when you allow every part of your emotional world to be acknowledged with honesty and compassion. It appears when fear can be listened to without taking control, when sadness can be felt without becoming overwhelming, and when anger can reveal boundaries that deserve protection.

Rather than fighting against your emotions, you begin working with them.

You learned that emotional safety is the foundation that makes this work possible. Without stability in the nervous system, reflection becomes difficult and insight remains distant. By slowing down, grounding yourself, and creating supportive environments, you make space for emotional understanding to grow.

You also explored the idea of reparenting, the practice of offering yourself the validation, protection, and encouragement that may have been missing earlier in life. Instead of relying only on external approval, you begin developing a compassionate relationship with yourself.

This inner relationship gradually becomes a source of strength.

When the adult part of you responds to fear with patience or to mistakes with understanding, the emotional system learns that vulnerability does not lead to rejection. The inner child begins experiencing the care that once felt uncertain.

The work of rewriting core beliefs helped reveal how deeply assumptions about worth, safety, and love influence everyday decisions. Beliefs such as "I am not enough" or "I must earn connection" often guide choices quietly in the background.

By examining these beliefs and replacing them with grounded, evidence-based truths, you begin reshaping the emotional lens through which life is interpreted.

This change does not occur through affirmation alone. It grows through repeated experiences that support a new understanding of yourself and your relationships.

You saw how this transformation extends into relationships as well.

When emotional wounds remain unexamined, they often drive patterns of overgiving, withdrawal, defensiveness, or fear of vulnerability. Healing allows those patterns to shift. Communication becomes clearer, boundaries become healthier, and connections become more balanced.

Relationships stop repeating old pain and begin offering opportunities for growth.

Along the way, you also confronted an important truth: healing is rarely a straight line.

Setbacks, moments of discouragement, and temporary returns to familiar patterns are part of the process. These experiences do not erase progress. Often they reveal the next layer of understanding waiting to be explored.

Learning to face setbacks with reflection, repair, and recommitment transforms them from obstacles into teachers.

As this journey comes to a close, one message becomes especially important.

Insight alone does not create lasting change. Transformation happens through practice.

Many people wait for the perfect moment to apply what they have learned. They imagine that once they feel completely ready, confident, or certain, they will begin acting differently.

In truth, readiness grows through action.

Small repeated choices create the foundation of emotional freedom. Each time you pause to notice what you are feeling, you strengthen awareness. Each time you regulate your nervous system during a stressful moment, you strengthen resilience. Each time you communicate honestly or protect a boundary, you reinforce self-respect.

These moments may appear ordinary when viewed individually.

But over time they shape the direction of your life.

Daily emotional check-ins keep awareness active. Repairing misunderstandings strengthens relationships. Reflecting on experiences deepens understanding. Practicing relational honesty transforms connection from obligation into authenticity.

These practices do not require perfection.

There will be days when awareness feels clear and others when old patterns briefly reappear. The important thing is not flawless performance but continued willingness to return to the work.

Healing becomes sustainable when it is woven into the rhythm of everyday life.

Ultimately, emotional freedom is not defined by the absence of difficulty. It is defined by the presence of self-trust.

Self-trust grows when you know that your emotions can be understood rather than feared. It grows when you believe that your needs deserve attention and your voice deserves expression.

Emotional freedom also includes flexibility.

Instead of reacting automatically to familiar triggers, you develop the ability to pause and choose your response. You learn that vulnerability can coexist with strength and that boundaries can coexist with compassion.

Perhaps most importantly, emotional freedom creates deeper peace.

This peace does not depend on controlling every circumstance. It comes from knowing that whatever life brings—joy, disappointment, uncertainty—you have the capacity to meet it with awareness and care.

The journey toward wholeness does not end here.

Growth continues through the relationships you nurture, the routines you practice, and the conversations you have with yourself. Each interaction offers an opportunity to strengthen the awareness and compassion you have cultivated.

You may notice that the way you see yourself has already begun to change. Instead of viewing your history as a source of limitation, you may begin recognizing the resilience that allowed you to reach this moment.

The parts of you that once carried pain also carried strength. They helped you survive experiences that were confusing, overwhelming, or lonely.

Now those same parts are being invited into a new relationship—one defined by understanding rather than judgment.

This is what it means to keep becoming whole.

Wholeness is not a final destination where growth stops. It is an ongoing process of returning to yourself with honesty and care. Each step you take toward awareness strengthens that connection.

As you continue forward, remember that healing does not require perfection or extraordinary circumstances. It grows through ordinary moments of courage: a truthful conversation, a compassionate thought, a boundary that protects your well-being.

These moments create a life that is no longer organized around old wounds but around the deeper truth of who you are.

And from that place of wholeness, emotional possibility expands.